W9-AHF-189

Helping Your Child Grow and Develop

Karen Zimmerman, Ph.D.
Professor, Family and Consumer Sciences Education
University of Wisconsin–Stout
Menomonie, Wisconsin

Publisher
The Goodheart-Willcox Company, Inc.
Tinley Park, Illinois

Copyright 2002

by

The Goodheart-Willcox Company, Inc.

All rights reserved. No part of this book may be reproduced, stored in a retrieval system, or transmitted in any form or by any means, electronic, mechanical, photocopying, recording, or otherwise, without the prior written permission of The Goodheart-Willcox Company, Inc. Manufactured in the United States of America.

Library of Congress Catalog Card Number 2001033352

ISBN-13: 978-1-56637-852-9
ISBN-10: 1-56637-852-4

2 3 4 5 6 7 8 9 10   01   07 06

Library of Congress Cataloging-in-Publication Data

Zimmerman, Karen
Helping your child grow and develop / Karen Zimmerman.
    p. cm. -- (Transitions)
ISBN 1-56637-852-4
    1. Teenage pregnancy. 2. Teenage mothers. 3. Child care. 4. Parenting 5. Infants--Care.
I. Title. II. Transitions (Tinley Park, Ill.)

RG525 .Z56 2001
649'.1--dc21   2001033352

Introduction

From the first moment you hold your new baby, you will want to be the best parent you can be. In fact, you may have started thinking of yourself as a parent even before your baby was born. At the same time, you may feel overwhelmed by all there is to learn about being a parent.

You will have many questions, some of which include the following:

- ☛ What does your baby want and need, and how can you best meet these needs?
- ☛ What changes can you expect in growth and development from birth to age three?
- ☛ How can you protect your child's health and promote safety?
- ☛ How should you guide your child?
- ☛ What should you look for when choosing a child care provider?

Helping Your Child Grow and Develop will help answer these questions in a language that is interesting and easy to understand. This book provides practical information for young mothers and fathers about how to provide the care their children need. It's important to remember both parents can nurture a child and encourage his or her growth and development. Even if you and your baby's other parent are not together, each of you still has much to offer your child.

Your baby may be a girl or a boy. To make the chapters easier to read, we have referred to your baby in some sections as <u>he</u> and in other sections as <u>she</u>. We hope this will also help you relate to the chapters in a personal way as you think about your child. Do all you can to parent with love and keep your child safe and healthy!

4

Acknowledgments

We would like to thank the following professionals who reviewed this text and provided valuable input:

Cathy Allison
GRADS Coordinator
Auburn Career Center
Concord, Ohio

Dawn Gale Aspacher
Parent Educator
Child and Family Resources, Inc.
  The Center for Adolescent
  Parents
Tucson, Arizona

JoAnn J. Bartek
FCS Teacher/Director,
  Student Parent Team SCLC
Lincoln High School
Lincoln, Nebraska

Martha Hamdani-Swain
former Program Coordinator,
Pregnancy Education and
  Parenting Program
Jack Yates High School
Houston, Texas

Sheree M. Moser
FCS Department Chair and
District Assistant
Lincoln High School
Lincoln, Nebraska

Sara McDonald Rohar
Project Director,
Young Mother's Program
Birmingham City Schools
Birmingham, Alabama

Table of Contents

Chapter 4:
Keeping Your Baby Healthy and Safe 75

Chapter 5:
Your Toddler's Physical Development and Needs 99

Chapter 6:
Your Toddler's Intellectual,
Social, and Emotional Development 126

Chapter 9:
Choosing Child Care 200

Glossary 230

Index 236

Transitions:
A Series for Pregnant and Parenting Teens

Understanding Your Changing Life
by Linda G. Smock, CFCS

This two-part book addresses the transitions teen pregnancy and parenting bring. Topics include: self-esteem; values, goals, options, and decisions related to pregnancy; adjusting to parenthood; communication; relationships with family, friends and co-parent; partner relationships and sexual decisions; birth control; STDs; and crises in relationships.

Your New Baby
by Angela M. Nicoletti, RNC, WHNP

By telling teens what to expect, this book reduces the fear and mystery of pregnancy and childbirth. Topics include: prenatal development; eating, exercise, and health care recommendations; preparations for parenting; labor and delivery; the postpartum period; and newborn care.

Helping Your Child Grow and Develop
by Karen Zimmerman, Ph.D.

This book suggests practical ways for teen parents to promote development; identify and meet a child's needs; provide a safe, loving environment; guide behavior; and choose quality child care. Developmental Milestones charts describe each area of development for infants and toddlers.

Building Your Future
by Sally R. Campbell

This book helps teen parents learn to manage their lives, their families, and their futures. It explains how to find help, handle legal issues, manage money and resources; shop wisely; use credit and financial accounts; set goals, and become a successful worker.

Chapter 1
Your Baby's
Physical Development

Infants grow and change daily. As a newborn, your baby is helpless, depending upon you to meet all his needs. During infancy (the period from birth to the first birthday), your baby will grow and develop in many ways. Over the next few months, he will become more skilled in his movements. He will be better able to relate to others and show his feelings. Toward the end of this first year, your baby will start learning to walk and talk.

As a parent, it is your job to meet your baby's needs. He counts on you to take care of him! See Figure 1-1. It's your job to guide your baby's development. Development refers to gradual changes that take place over time as a result of growth. Your baby grows and changes in many ways. By learning about child development, you can know what to expect from your baby. This will help you offer the right experiences so he can reach his full potential. You can also learn how to meet his many needs.

Types of Development

Your baby is amazing! She grows and changes rapidly. These changes happen in four main areas—physical, intellectual, social, and emotional. As an infant, she will make great strides in each area. She will keep developing in these four ways throughout her life.

Physical development means change in the body and its abilities. As your baby's body develops, she will be able to do more things. An example is learning to walk. She will go through many changes before taking her first step.

Intellectual development means progress in the mind and its thinking abilities. As your baby's mind develops, she will be able to think in more complex ways. An example is learning to talk.

Social development means learning to relate to other people. First, your baby will learn she's a person separate from you. As she grows, she will learn even more about relationships. An example is learning to play with others.

Emotional development means learning to express and handle feelings. As your baby grows, she will learn to identify what she is feeling and share it with you. An example is learning to express joy by smiling.

Your infant needs you to care for him and see that his needs are met.

Principles of Development

As you study development, it is good to learn a few basic principles. These principles show that most children develop in ways that are alike.

- ☛ Development is continuous. From birth to death, people continually grow and change. At every age, development occurs. Throughout life, people develop physically, intellectually, socially, and emotionally.
- ☛ Development follows a set order. All over the world, children go through the stages of development in the same order. This is true whether they live in Texas, China, California, Brazil, or Kenya. For example, children sit before they crawl. They crawl before they stand alone. They stand before walking and walk before running.

   Learning to talk also follows a developmental order. Your baby starts by making sounds. A few months later, he learns to say ball. As a toddler, he will use two-word sentences, such as throw ball. When he is three years old, he will form even longer sentences.

☞ The rate of development changes over time. Infancy is the most rapid period of development in a person's life. Your baby will grow and change more quickly now than at any other age. See Figure 1-2. His rate of physical growth will slow during the school-age years. It will increase again in the early teen years. Even this rate is not as fast as development in infancy, though. Adults are also still developing, but this occurs at a much slower rate.

☞ People develop at different rates. No two children are alike. Each child grows and develops at his own rate. Three children may start to walk at three different ages. This is normal. Your child may develop faster or slower than other children you know. As you study child development, you will learn average age ranges for certain changes. Your baby may fall within these ranges. He may also be a little ahead of or behind them. Don't worry unless your child develops much more slowly than the average.

1-2 The rate of development changes over time—it's much faster in infancy than at any other time in life.

☞ All types of development are connected. Development is complex. Your baby doesn't develop just physically one week and just mentally the next. Each type is connected. His body, mind, and emotions work together. Changes happen in each area at the same time. Each change affects other types of development. To learn about development, though, it's easiest to study one type at a time.

☞ The body develops from head to toe. Development occurs in a head-to-toe pattern. At birth, your baby's head is about one-fourth of his total body length. His chest and legs are relatively short. As he grows, his body proportions will change. His chest and legs will grow at a faster rate than his head. When he's an adult, his head will be about one-eighth of his total body length (height). His legs will account for almost half his height. Your baby also develops muscle control in this head-to-toe pattern. Figure 1-3 gives an example of this head-to-toe pattern in muscle control during the first year.

☞ The body develops from the trunk outward. Your baby develops from the center of his body outward. Refer to Figure 1-3 again to see how development moves from the center outward. Your baby's center muscles are those of his trunk and shoulders. He learns to use these muscles first. One way he uses them is in learning to roll over. Then your baby learns to control his arms. He uses his arms to reach, crawl, and pull himself to a stand. Later, your baby gains control of his hands and finally, his fingers. He uses these muscles to hold, grasp, and handle an object or toy.

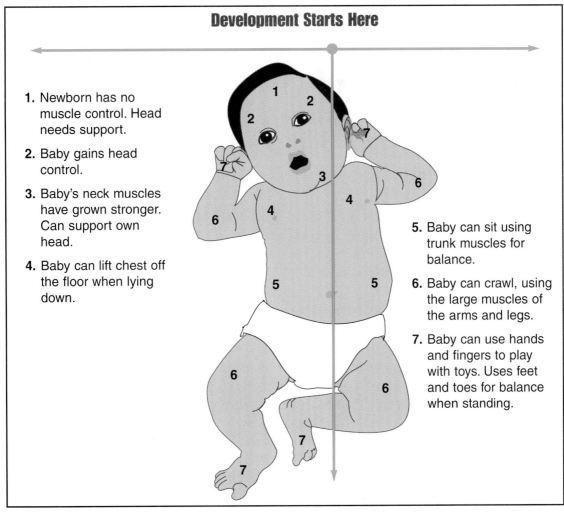

Development Starts Here

1. Newborn has no muscle control. Head needs support.

2. Baby gains head control.

3. Baby's neck muscles have grown stronger. Can support own head.

4. Baby can lift chest off the floor when lying down.

5. Baby can sit using trunk muscles for balance.

6. Baby can crawl, using the large muscles of the arms and legs.

7. Baby can use hands and fingers to play with toys. Uses feet and toes for balance when standing.

1-3 As you can see from this diagram, development moves along the arrows—from head to toe and from the center outward.

☛ Both heredity and environment affect development. The sum of the traits parents pass to their children is called heredity. Your baby inherited certain traits from each of his parents. Some of these are hair color, eye color, body build, and height. Your baby inherited some physical and mental abilities from each of you, too. Heredity can also include certain health conditions that are passed down through families.

Environment means all the effects from your baby's surroundings. This includes your home, family, and community. As his parent, you play a key role. How you care for your baby affects his development. Without good food, plenty of rest, hygiene (cleanliness), and loving attention, he can't be his best. With all these needs met, he can grow and learn well.

You may wonder which has a bigger effect—heredity or environment. Opinions vary on this point. Research suggests that each is important. Both affect your child's growth and development.

Your Baby's Physical Growth

As an infant, your child grows very quickly and changes at a fast rate. She becomes longer and gains weight. Her skeleton, skull, and brain grow. A first tooth will likely appear. This is an exciting first year for physical growth!

Average growth ranges are a general guideline about what to expect, but your baby is an individual. She will grow at her own pace. At any given age, she may be longer, shorter, heavier, or lighter than average. This is most likely normal. If you have any concerns about your baby's growth, share them with her health care provider. This person has the training and experience to know whether there is a problem.

Length

At birth, babies average 19 to 21 inches in length. Your baby will grow much longer during his first year. His skeleton is growing rapidly.

He will probably grow 9 ½ to 10 inches longer by his first birthday. Most babies are about 30 inches long at one year. See Figure 1-4.

Babies grow in spurts. During a growth spurt, your baby may grow as much as half an inch longer within 24 hours! Then growth slows again to its normal rate. A week or longer will pass between growth spurts. Sometimes growth spurts may be as long as two months apart.

Just before a growth spurt starts, your baby may seem fussy, restless, and very hungry. This is normal. Many changes are taking place in his body. Be patient with your baby during these times. Soon he will be his usual self again.

Weight

Most infants gain weight quickly. At birth, the average baby weighs 7 ½ pounds. Within the first days after birth, your baby's weight may drop slightly. This is normal. However, she should be back to her birthweight when she's a week old. If it

Average Length and Weight During the First Year

Age	Length		Weight	
	Girls	Boys	Girls	Boys
Birth	19¾ in.	20 in.	7¼ lb.	7½ lb.
3 months	23½ in.	24 in.	12 lb.	13¼ lb.
6 months	26 in.	26½ in.	16 lb.	17 lb.
9 months	27¾ in.	28 in.	18¾ lb.	20 lb.
12 months	29¼ in.	30 in.	21 lb.	22¼ lb.

1-4 Many babies almost triple their birthweight in the first year. They grow 1½ times longer, too. Keep in mind these figures are just averages.

seems your baby is not gaining enough weight, do not hesitate to call her health care provider. You can take the baby in to be weighed, and the provider can check her progress. This can reassure you everything is okay.

By 5 months, your baby's weight will likely double to 15 pounds. By 12 months, she may triple her birthweight, averaging 21 or 22 pounds. Most often, boys are a little heavier than girls. Refer again to Figure 1-4 for more details.

Your baby needs to gain weight and add body fat. This body fat helps her keep warm. Most babies have a plump look when they're about nine months old. This is normal for their age. Your baby will slim down when she becomes a toddler.

Teeth

On average, a baby's first tooth appears at about six months of age. A few babies are born with one or two teeth. Some get a first tooth as early as three months. Others don't have any teeth until after they're a year old. After the first tooth appears, new ones will come in every month or two. The bottom front teeth usually come in first.

Your baby may be cranky and his gums may be sore when a tooth is pushing through. He may fuss more than usual and be harder to comfort. Your baby may drool a lot and need to suck or chew more. However, teething does not cause fever, vomiting, or diarrhea. If your baby shows any of these signs, have a health care provider check him.

To relieve teething pain, you can soothe your baby's gums with a chilled bagel or an ice cube wrapped in a clean washcloth. This cold, hard object will feel good on his gums. You can also ask your baby's health care provider for advice. Some providers may suggest teething rings, while others do not. (Some studies say teething rings may be dangerous for babies.) Other providers may suggest the use of a numbing gel for the baby's mouth.

Your newborn's gums need care. When your baby's teeth start coming in, they will need care, too. To care for your baby's gums and teeth, use the following guidelines:

- ☛ Wipe teeth and gums with a gauze pad or clean washcloth after each feeding or at least twice a day.
- ☛ Do not put the baby to bed with a bottle.
- ☛ Avoid giving your baby sugar-coated foods.
- ☛ Do not put anything sweet on the pacifier.

Using these tips will remove sugars, acids, and bacteria from the mouth. It will keep his gums clean and prevent cavities in his baby teeth. Starting early will also help you and your baby grow used to tooth care as a part of your routine.

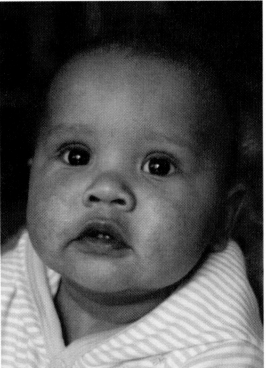

Billie Hainsey

Baby teeth are important. See Figure 1-5. They hold the spacing for permanent teeth. These teeth are also needed for learning correct speech. When your baby has a couple of teeth, you can give him a toothbrush of his own. Buy two child-sized toothbrushes with soft bristles. Give one to the baby so he can play with it and get used to it.

Once your baby is comfortable with his toothbrush, start using the second one to brush his teeth. At brushing times, give your baby his toothbrush and use the other one for the actual brushing. Use only a pea-sized amount of toothpaste and discourage your child from swallowing it. Swallowing large amounts of fluoride (a mineral in toothpaste) is not good for children.

 Baby teeth are important to the development of permanent teeth, so be sure to take care of them.

Avoid putting your baby to bed with a bottle. Suppose he falls asleep with a bottle in his mouth. Formula, breast milk, or juice will leak from the bottle even after he stops actively sucking. The sugars, acids, and bacteria in the fluid will pool in his mouth, which can cause a severe form of tooth decay. If your baby ever falls asleep with a bottle in his mouth, remove it right away. If he shows a need to suck for comfort, you can offer a pacifier instead.

Letting a baby carry a bottle with him all day can also cause tooth decay. Give your baby a bottle when he is thirsty and take it away when his thirst seems satisfied. Limit the amount of sugary drinks you give an infant and offer water more often.

Head Growth

Your baby's head will also grow during the first year. Her head's circumference (distance around) will increase by 4 to 5 inches. At your baby's checkups, her doctor may measure this growth and tell you whether her measurement is average.

A newborn has soft spots between skull bones. These soft spots allow her head to pass through the birth canal. They also give her brain room to grow. (An infant's brain will double its weight by age two.) Protect your baby's soft spots from injury. Gentle washing and touching of the soft spots will not hurt her, though. Her skull will become harder as the bones fuse (grow together). By age two, her skull will be completely fused. The soft spots will have disappeared.

Brain Development

Your newborn's brain is his most vital organ. It controls all his bodily functions. At birth, the brain contains 100 billion cells called neurons. These neurons create electrical charges to send messages to other parts of the brain. These messages command the brain's work. They allow your child to think, learn, and do.

To send and receive these messages, a pathway is needed between the neurons. Compare this to the Internet. You and your friend may each have a computer. Without the needed connections, however, you can't send e-mail to your friend. The message can't get through. In the brain, the neurons must also be connected to one another. At birth, 50 trillion of these connections have been made. Each connection is called a synapse. Synapses let neurons communicate with one another.

The brain works well if enough connections are made. With the right kind of help, the brain can make as many as 1,000 trillion connections by age one. This is where you, the parent, come in. The care you give your child can greatly influence the number of synapses, or connections, his brain makes. You are the single most important person in determining your baby's future brain potential!

How can you affect this process? The brain only makes the connections it is "told" to make. Many of your actions can tell your baby's brain to make connections. Together, these actions are called stimulation. When you stimulate your baby's brain in some way, a connection will be made. By repeating this stimulation, the connection will grow stronger. It will become a permanent part of your child's brain.

Your influence is most vital in your baby's first three years of life. Your baby needs to eat well, play, and be touched often. Offer your baby warm, consistent care that makes him feel safe and encourages him to learn. Hold, cuddle, and talk to him often. Early nutrition and relationships mold the brain. Positive stimulation helps his brain grow and form connections. A list of activities you can provide to stimulate your baby's brain is given in Figure 1-6. What other ideas can you think of to stimulate your baby's brain?

Ways to Stimulate Your Baby's Brain

- ❖ Provide loving care and meet your baby's needs.
- ❖ Touch, kiss, and hold your baby.
- ❖ Protect the baby from abuse, high amounts of stress, and negative effects.
- ❖ Offer the baby chances to develop each skill within its window of opportunity.
- ❖ Help your baby explore the environment safely.
- ❖ Allow the baby to move about and practice motor skills.
- ❖ Praise your baby for attempts and successes.
- ❖ Talk to your baby and repeat your baby's sounds.
- ❖ Read to your baby and look at age-appropriate books together.
- ❖ Give the baby interesting objects to look at and play with.
- ❖ Play music. Sing and dance with your baby.
- ❖ Play games. Hiding and peek-a-boo build the memory.

1-6 Your baby's brain develops most rapidly in the first three years. By providing stimulation, you can help your baby's brain reach its potential.

Negative influences can have an effect, too. These effects can harm his brain the most in the first three years of life. A lack of good food, touching, or stimulation can keep his brain from reaching its full size. It might be 20 to 30 percent smaller than average for his age. High levels of stress and fear are also a danger. They can change the way his brain is wired. Abuse and neglect can prevent connections from forming in some areas of the brain. Any of these negative effects could rob your baby of some of his future brain potential. The effects can last a lifetime.

Early learning experiences are also crucial. Your baby's brain has certain times in which it is best able to learn certain skills. These times are called windows of opportunity. For example, the window of opportunity for motor skills is one to five years. During this time, your baby has the best chance of learning to move his body. After this time, it will be much harder for him to learn new motor skills. In a few cases, a skill can't be learned at all after its window has passed.

You can use these windows to help your child maximize his brain's potential. Provide stimulation to encourage him to develop a skill within its window. Offer him activities to build synapses (connections) in his brain. These connections will help him perform new skills. Practicing a new skill will strengthen the synapse. This will make the skill a permanent part of his brain. (After 10 years, the brain weeds out synapses that are never or rarely used. It gets rid of these to make more room for the stronger synapses that are used more often.)

Your Baby's Senses

Your baby has the same senses as you do. She can see, hear, smell, taste, and respond to touch. She uses her senses to learn and gather information about the world. See Figure 1-7. By knowing what she can do, you can help her in this process.

Sight

During the first few weeks of life, your baby sees best at a distance of 8 to 12 inches. This is just about how far your face is from him when you hold or feed him. Your baby likes to look at your face. He likes to see other faces, too.

Your baby also likes to look at the following:

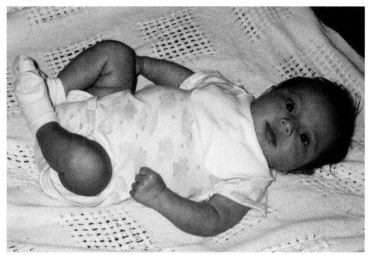

Esther Jacome

- ☛ <u>bright colors</u>
- ☛ patterns rather than plain colors
- ☛ contrasts between dark and light colors, such as a bull's-eye or checkerboard pattern
- ☛ shiny things
- ☛ moving objects

 1-7 Your baby learns by using her senses. She often watches and listens to you.

Just like you, your baby gets bored if he sees the same things all the time. Give him plenty of interesting things to see. You can hang a mobile from the side (not the top) of your newborn's crib. This is easier for him to see. Newborns naturally turn their heads to the side when they are lying down. When your baby is awake, change his position sometimes so he gets a different view. Move him to another room or turn him around in his infant seat or swing.

By <u>three months</u> of age, your baby's vision is more like yours. At this age, he can see farther. He can also move his hands to swipe at objects. Now you will want to move the mobiles from the side of his crib. They might be dangerous to him there. Instead, put them over the top of the crib out of his reach. You can also make brightly colored pictures or posters to hang on the walls. Change these often. Your baby needs lots of visual stimulation. When he's six months old, your baby can change <u>positions</u> on his own to look at interesting objects.

Hearing

At birth, your baby has <u>excellent</u> hearing. She can also react to what she hears. Your baby likes it when you to talk to her. It comforts her and teaches her, too. Her brain growth is stimulated by hearing your voice. She also learns about language. Your baby prefers higher-pitched, gentle voices. She started to hear your voice even before she was born and can recognize your voice from <u>birth.</u>

You can use sounds to soothe your baby. Play soft music to calm her when she's fussy. Sing to her and read aloud. Protect your baby from <u>loud sounds</u> that might damage her hearing. These sounds can scare her, too.

A <u>hearing problem</u> can limit your baby's learning. Use the questions in Figure 1-8 to check your baby's hearing. If you think she may have a hearing problem, tell her health care provider at once. It's important to treat hearing problems early.

Smell

Your baby has a keen sense of smell at birth. He can also react to what he smells. Your baby can recognize you by your unique <u>body scent.</u> If you nurse him, he also knows you by the smell of your <u>milk.</u>

Checking Your Baby's Hearing

Ages 3 to 6 Months
* Does your child awaken to your voice?
* Does your child become quiet when you talk?

Ages 7 to 10 Months
* Does your child turn her head and shoulders toward a sound even when she can't see what is happening? (ringing phone, mewing cat, rustling papers)
* Does your child respond when you call his name?

Ages 11 to 15 Months
* Does your child point to or look at objects you talk about?
* Does your child cry when it thunders?
* Does your child make sounds when you talk to her?

You can use these questions to check your baby's hearing. If you think there might be a problem, let her health care provider know right away.

He may also recognize other family members by their special scents. Your baby will cry and turn away from strong and harsh odors.

Taste

Your baby can tell the difference between tastes as a newborn. She is born with a preference for sweet tastes. This motivates her to eat—her milk or formula has a sweet taste. Most babies don't like sour or bitter tastes. Since their taste buds are much more sensitive than an adult's, they may dislike foods with strong tastes.

Touch

Being touched is very important to your baby. He enjoys being held close and cuddled. This helps him feel secure. Babies who are held more often cry less than other babies. Touch and hold your baby often. This will teach him that you care. Give him lots of hugs, kisses, and strokes. He can't receive too much love and attention at this age. No matter what others may tell you, you can't spoil a young baby!

Your baby learns from being touched. He senses how you feel about him by the way you handle him. Touching and holding your baby stimulates his brain. It helps his brain make needed connections that will help him think and learn.

Babies also learn through touching. As your baby gets older, he will learn more about you by patting your face or grabbing your hair. Give him objects of different textures to feel. He may enjoy feeling a blanket, cuddling a soft toy, or splashing in the bath water. This stimulates his brain, too.

Your baby may also learn about textures by mouthing objects. You may wonder why almost every object your baby can grab onto ends up in his mouth. This is how he explores his world. Letting him mouth safe, clean objects with you nearby will help him learn. Watch him closely to be sure he doesn't handle objects that are dangerous, dirty, or small enough to present a risk of choking.

Coordination of Large and Small Muscles

Physical development occcurs at a rapid pace in the first year. Your baby's brain, senses, and muscles work together to control her movements. This is called coordination. Your baby will become much more coordinated in this first year.

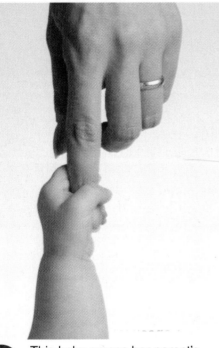

1-9 This baby grasps her parent's hand. At birth, she can do this by reflex, but as grows, she can grasp on her own.

Your infant will first start to gain co-ordination in her large muscles. The large muscles are those of the neck, trunk, arms, and legs. The skills she will learn using these muscles are called large motor skills. Lifting her head and chest is a large motor skill. Other examples are rolling over, sitting, crawling, pulling to a stand, and starting to walk.

Your baby will gain coordination in her small muscles, too. The muscles of her eyes, hands, feet, fingers, and toes are her small muscles. Skills using these muscles are called small motor skills. These include learning to reach for and grasp objects and toys. See Figure 1-9. This takes hand-eye coordination. When she's six months old, your baby will be able to pick up finger foods and put them in her mouth. By her first birthday, she will be able to scribble holding a crayon and drink holding a cup.

Understanding Developmental Milestones

Over the next year, your baby will accomplish many tasks and learn many skills. When he learns something new, this is a developmental milestone. It means your baby has reached a higher level in his development.

For years, experts have studied babies to learn more about how they develop. This research shows the average age at which most infants reach a certain milestone. For example, the average age for

starting to sit without support is six
months. Keep in mind this is just an
average—about half of all six-month-
olds will have mastered the skill and
half will not. You should be concerned
only if your child shows a significant
delay in reaching a milestone.

By studying child development, you
can learn what to expect as your child
grows. This can help you form more
realistic expectations of him. You can
better predict his readiness for
certain tasks. This means you won't do
things for your child he is ready to
handle for himself. It also means you
won't push him to learn certain skills
before his body is ready. (Either of
these approaches can frustrate both
you and your child. They can also
damage your child's self-esteem and
hinder his development.)

 If you often put your child on his
tummy in a safe place, he will soon
learn to crawl.

When you know what skills your
child will soon develop, you can guide him more effectively. By
offering activities to promote these skills, you can encourage
your child's independence. If you offer him chances to succeed,
you can also help build his self-esteem. See Figure 1-10.

Knowing the averages for various milestones can reassure
you about your child's development. Being aware of these
averages can alert you if a significant delay exists. This will
allow you to seek needed help for your child right away.

Finally, studying child development can help you better
understand your child. You will learn that many of his behaviors
are normal and help him learn about the world. This can
encourage you to be patient rather than being frustrated by
these behaviors or taking them personally.

See the <u>Developmental Milestones</u> chart at the end of this chapter. This chart describes the milestones for physical development that will occur in your baby's first year. Keep in mind the ages given in this chart are only averages. Ask your child's health care provider any questions you may have about your child's development.

☞ You are the most important person in your baby's life. It is up to you to care for your baby and meet his needs.

☞ Development means how your child changes over time as a result of growth. Your child will experience changes in all four types of development.

☞ The principles of development are basic ideas that can guide your study. Understanding these principles that apply to all people can help you learn more about your baby.

☞ Physical development is rapid in the first year. Most babies grow 9½ to 10 inches longer and triple their birthweights. Their heads grow 4 to 5 inches larger around and the soft spots start to close. Your baby will likely have at least one tooth in the first year.

☞ Your baby's brain is her most vital organ. Its neurons need good care and stimulation to help them form needed connections called synapses. They enable her to think, learn, and do. You are the biggest influence on your child's growing brain.

☞ Your baby has the same senses you do. At birth, he can see, but his vision isn't very well developed. The senses of hearing, taste, and smell work well. Your baby also learns through touching and being touched.

☞ Coordination is the work your baby's brain, senses, and muscles do to control body movements. In infancy, your baby will gain coordination in her large and small muscles. You can help her develop both large and small motor skills.

☞ Your baby will have many accomplishments, which are called developmental milestones. Reaching a milestone means your baby has reached a higher level of development. Learning when these milestones often occur will help you know what to expect from your baby.

Birth to 12 Months

As your newborn, I

❖ move by reflex. My movements are not yet voluntary.

❖ have a grasping reflex. I instinctively grasp an object with a firm grip when you place it in the palm of my hand.

❖ have a rooting reflex. I instinctively begin to suck when anything touches my lips or cheeks.

❖ have a startle reflex. I instinctively change my position in response to loud sounds or sudden changes.

❖ need support for my head. It bobs forward or backward if not supported.

❖ blink at bright lights.

❖ keep my hands closed in fists most of the time.

As your one-month-old, I

❖ still have mostly reflex movements, but I can make some voluntary ones.

❖ hold my head somewhat steadier. I still need you to support my head when you lift me, though.

❖ can raise my head above a flat surface. I will gradually hold it up for longer and longer periods of time.

❖ thrust out my arms and legs in play.

❖ can follow light or a bright object with my eyes.

As your two-month-old, I

❖ make more and more voluntary movements. My reflex actions are fading.

❖ can lift my head and chest when lying on my stomach, but I can't hold this position very long.

❖ turn my head while lying on my back.

❖ have better muscle tone.

❖ cycle my arms and legs smoothly. I can use this motion in my play.

❖ look at objects longer and more closely than I did before. I can follow a moving object for a few seconds if it is close enough.

❖ can make more facial expressions and sounds.

As your three-month-old, I

❖ use all voluntary movements.

❖ have more head control than before.

❖ can lift my head and chest for about 10 seconds when lying on my stomach. I lean on my elbows for support.

❖ turn my head to find the source of the sounds I hear.

❖ like to sit when propped with pillows.

❖ keep my hands open most of the time now. I grasp objects with my open hands.

❖ like to hold and shake a rattle.

❖ can look around, follow objects with my eyes, and look from object to object.

(Continued)

29

Developmental Milestones: Physical Development

Birth to 12 Months

As your four-month-old, I

✤ can hold my head steady when you pick me up.

✤ turn my head in all directions while I am lying down.

✤ may roll from side to back or back to side.

✤ can sit with assistance in your arms.

✤ splash and kick in the bathtub.

✤ enjoy playing with my hands and swiping at objects. My aim is still unsteady, so I often miss my target.

✤ like to hold interesting objects. I can even pull a dangling object toward me.

✤ am interested in smells and know the difference between some of them.

As your five-month-old, I

✤ lift my head and shoulders when lying on my back.

✤ can sit with support for 15 to 30 minutes. Be sure to watch me, though! I can still fall.

✤ roll from stomach to back and from back to stomach. I like to rock, scoot, and twist in all directions.

✤ have a steadier grasp. I can hold an object between my index and second fingers.

✤ grasp objects with my whole palm and all five fingers like a scoop.

✤ grab at every object within my reach. I aim well now.

✤ bring my feet to my hands so I can play with them. I sometimes like to put my toes in my mouth.

✤ can hold my bottle with two hands.

As your six-month-old, I

✤ can sit alone briefly. My balance is better when sitting now.

✤ may feel the urge to stand with support.

✤ may creep when lying on my stomach. This means I propel myself with my legs and steer with my arms.

✤ can hold an object in one hand and transfer it to my other hand.

✤ pick things up, shake them, and listen to the sound they make when I drop them.

✤ explore objects with my mouth.

✤ might start teething. My first tooth may come in now.

✤ easily grasp finger foods, such as crackers. I have strong taste preferences now.

As your seven-month-old, I

✤ push myself forward by rocking, wiggling, or squirming.

✤ get up on my hands and knees so I can rock back and forth.

✤ sit unassisted for longer periods now.

✤ may be able to sit from a lying position.

✤ can pull to a standing position and support my own weight.

✤ may get my second tooth.

✤ like to pick up small objects and put them in my mouth.

✤ can hold an object in each hand and bang them together.

(Continued)

30

Birth to 12 Months

As your eight-month-old, I

❖ can crawl now. I may crawl with an object in one hand.

❖ can stand without holding on if I'm leaning against something.

❖ use furniture to pull myself to a stand. I may need your help to get back down.

❖ explore everything, since I can move around now.

❖ grasps objects in my fingers.

❖ begin to eat using my fingers.

❖ have learned to point to objects and will look where you have pointed.

As your nine-month-old, I

❖ stand on my own.

❖ cruise (take sideways steps while holding onto a piece of furniture).

❖ start to climb on everything.

❖ may try to crawl up and down stairs.

❖ can vary my speed and turn around while crawling.

❖ pick up small things by bringing my thumb and index finger together.

❖ can handle two objects at the same time, one with each hand.

❖ may wave bye-bye.

As your ten-month-old, I

❖ walk while holding onto both of your hands.

❖ get into and out of chairs.

❖ delight in grasping objects between my thumb and first two fingers.

❖ find many little objects and put them in my mouth.

❖ pick up larger objects.

❖ can carry two small objects in the same hand.

❖ am able to voluntarily release an object. I like to practice dropping and throwing objects.

❖ may show you that I prefer to use one hand more than the other.

As your eleven-month-old, I

❖ take a few steps on my own with confidence. I may suddenly lose my balance and sit with a thud.

❖ lower myself from a standing position without falling. I may lean over while standing against a support.

❖ may climb out of my crib now.

❖ combine crawling and walking.

❖ may stand on my toes.

❖ turn book pages, but not always one at a time.

❖ can place a small object inside a bigger one. I take lids off boxes and put things inside.

As your twelve-month-old, I

❖ may begin to walk alone. (The average age is from 9 and 16 months for walking alone.)

❖ easily lower myself to a sitting position.

❖ may insist on feeding myself.

❖ may be able to take off some of my own clothes.

❖ like to hold a pencil or crayon and scribble.

❖ hold and drink from a cup.

❖ pick up large objects using both hands.

❖ have mastered the pincer grasp (gripping an object between my thumb and index finger).

Chapter 2
Your Baby's Food, Sleep, and Clothing Needs

Meeting your growing baby's food, sleep, and clothing needs is a challenge. Of course you want her to grow up healthy and strong. You may have many questions about caring for your baby. She's counting on you to meet her daily care needs. See Figure 2-1.

Providing nutritious foods, adequate sleep, and comfortable clothing is a big part of your job as a parent. Your baby needs you to choose the right foods for her. She needs good foods to give her a healthy start. Sleep is vital for both you and your baby. Using a bedtime routine helps your baby learn to sleep through the night. Her comfort and safety also depend upon the clothing you choose.

Meeting Your Baby's Changing Food Needs

One of your most important jobs as a parent is to give your baby nutritious foods. Good foods boost your child's early physical and intellectual development. Three-fourths of his brain growth will occur before age four. If he doesn't eat healthful foods in these early years, he may have a poorer memory and shorter attention span.

With a newborn, you should ask his health care provider how much to feed your baby and how often. For his first few weeks, you may have to wake him for feedings. If he refuses to eat, contact his provider and ask for guidance.

By the time he's a few weeks old, your baby will eat enough to satisfy his nutritional needs. If he doesn't want to eat a meal once in a while, it won't hurt him to miss it. There are days when your baby won't eat much. On other days, he'll eat a lot. This is especially common just before a growth spurt. What matters most is that your baby is healthy and grows properly. Ask his health care provider if you have any concerns. You can also take your baby in for weight checks to keep track of his growth.

Deniece Valenzuela, GRADS student at Artesia High School

Which foods you feed your baby will depend on his age. See Figure 2-2 for general guidelines about the best ages at which to introduce certain foods.

 Your baby depends on you to offer her healthy foods and provide her with a bedtime routine.

Birth to Four Months

For the first four to six months of life, your baby needs only breast milk or formula. Her digestive system isn't ready for solid foods. In fact, she hasn't yet developed the swallowing motion needed to eat solid foods. Newborns push their tongues out when they swallow. If you give your newborn solid foods, she might choke. This tongue movement will change as she grows older.

People used to think giving a baby solid foods early would help her sleep through the night. Research now shows this isn't true. A baby will start sleeping through the night when she is ready. Your baby is also more likely to develop food allergies if she is fed solid foods too early. In response to a food allergy, your baby might have an allergic reaction, such as vomiting, rash, or diarrhea.

Formula-fed infants may need to have a little water added to their diets. This is especially true in hot weather. Some experts advise half an ounce to two ounces of water between feedings. This amount should total four to eight ounces each day. Ask your baby's health care provider what he or she recommends.

Timetable for Offering New Foods

4 to 6 Months

Keep feeding breast milk or infant formula.

- ❖ Infant rice cereal (first)
- ❖ Infant oatmeal cereal
- ❖ Infant barley cereal

6 to 8 Months

Keep feeding infant cereals and breast milk or formula. Start introducing baby foods (prepared or homemade).

- ❖ Prepared baby foods—single-ingredient fruits and vegetables, one at a time
- ❖ Cooked fresh or frozen vegetables, strained or mashed—peas, carrots, beets, potatoes, sweet potatoes, and winter squash
- ❖ Strained or mashed fruits, fresh (if soft) or cooked—fresh bananas; cooked and peeled apples, peaches, pears, and plums
- ❖ Diluted fruit or vegetable juice from a cup

8 to 10 Months

Continue offering infant cereals and introduce infant wheat cereal. Continue offering baby foods (prepared or homemade). Start offering finger foods, one at a time.

- ❖ Grain group—dry toast, bagels, crackers, unsweetened dry cereal (whole-grain or enriched), cooked macaroni, noodles, and rice
- ❖ Vegetable group—cooked pieces of soft vegetables; vegetable juices
- ❖ Fruit group—soft, peeled fruit slices or pieces; unsweetened fruit juice
- ❖ Milk group—small pieces of mild cheeses
- ❖ Meat group-cooked and mashed beans; cooked boneless meat, poultry, and fish (small, tender pieces)

10 to 12 Months

Decrease number of feedings by bottle or breast, encourage self-feeding, encourage drinking from a cup.

- ❖ Mashed table foods
- ❖ Orange juice (at 12 months)
- ❖ Plain yogurt
- ❖ Cottage cheese
- ❖ Egg yolks (egg whites at 12 months)

2-2   Always ask your baby's health care provider before introducing foods to the baby's diet.

Four to Six Months

Most babies start solid foods between four to six months of age. Infant cereals are usually the first foods given. Right now, your baby is just learning how to eat. Breast milk or formula is still the main part of his diet, providing most of his nutrients. With your help, your baby may also be ready to start learning to drink from a cup. This may start as early as five months old.

Starting Solid Foods

Your baby will let you know when he needs more to eat. He may start to demand more milk or be displeased after each feeding. He might even demand another feeding. For example, a baby who has been sleeping all night may start to wake for a nighttime feeding. This might be a cue to start solid foods. Figure 2-3 lists other signs your baby may be ready for solid foods.

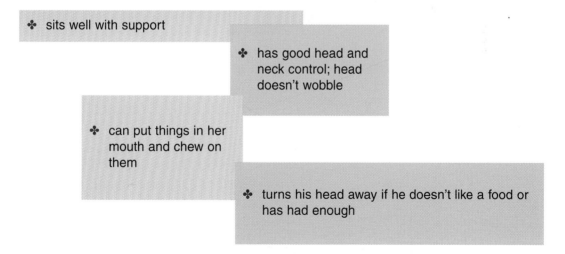

Is Your Baby Ready for Solid Foods?
The following are signs your baby may be ready for solid foods:

❧ sits well with support

❧ has good head and neck control; head doesn't wobble

❧ can put things in her mouth and chew on them

❧ turns his head away if he doesn't like a food or has had enough

2-3   It's important to be sure your baby is ready to start solid foods before you introduce them to her.

Ask your baby's health care provider before starting your baby on solid foods. The provider can tell you when to begin and which foods to try first. He or she can also describe the signs that may occur with an allergic reaction. If you notice these changes or have more questions, call the provider.

Infant Cereals

The term <u>solid foods</u> may be a little misleading. When you think of solid foods, an apple or a cracker may come to mind. These solid foods are firm and hard. The first solid foods in your baby's diet will be very smooth and runny. These foods are easiest for him to swallow and digest.

A good first food for your baby is rice cereal. Rice cereal is the kind least likely to cause an allergy. See Figure 2-4. When your baby does well with rice cereal, you can try oatmeal and then barley. Wait a few months to introduce wheat cereal and mixed cereals. These are more likely to cause allergies. Try these cereals at about 8 to 10 months of age.

Choosing the right cereal is important. Use dry infant cereals rather than jarred cereals. Dry cereals are more nutritious, and they also cost less. Select cereals that are made just for infants. These are made with your baby's nutritional needs in mind. Pick infant cereals that are iron-enriched. This means iron has been added. These cereals will meet his increasing needs for iron.

When starting cereals, pick a time when your baby is hungry, but not fussy. He will be most interested and patient then. Follow the tips on the next page for feeding infant cereals to your baby.

Billie Hainsey

2-4 Rice cereal is a perfect food for babies.

☞ Feed cereal to your baby with a small, narrow baby spoon. Do not mix cereal into his bottle. It is also not a good idea to use an infant feeder (tube with a plunger on one end and a nipple with a large hole on the other end). Your baby needs to learn to eat from a spoon even if it takes longer and is messier. An infant feeder also creates a risk of choking and other medical problems.

☞ In a small bowl, mix a tablespoon of rice cereal with about four to five tablespoons of breast milk or formula. The mixture should be about as thick and smooth as cream. After this first feeding, you can gradually decrease the amount of breast milk or formula you add.

☞ Sit your baby in your lap, an infant seat, or a high chair. Use a bib; expect a mess.

☞ Put the cereal in the middle of your baby's tongue. At first, your baby may push more food out of his mouth than he takes in. This is normal. Gently scrape the excess into his mouth.

Teaching your baby to eat solid foods takes patience. It takes time for him to learn to swallow. A couple of spoonfuls may be enough the first few feedings. Let your baby guide you. Never force your baby to eat more than he wants. Your baby will turn his head away when he has had enough. He might also whimper, cry, or look unhappy. Respect his signals and end the feeding. He may want more to eat at the next feeding.

When your baby starts eating solid foods, he will need to drink more water than before. Offer water several times a day during hot months. Your baby will lose fluid through sweating when he's hot.

Six to Eight Months

When your baby is six to eight months old, she will need to start eating more foods. See Figure 2-5 for tips on adding new foods to your baby's diet. At this age, your baby can eat smooth, semisolid foods. Most of these will be baby foods. You may buy these in the store or make them yourself. They will be about the thickness of pudding. Be sure these foods don't contain added sugar, salt, fat, or spices. These are not good for your baby.

Adding New Foods to Your Baby's Diet*

When your baby has learned to eat cereal, you can start other baby foods. Try fruits and vegetables next. When starting a new food,

❖ try each new food for three or four days. This gives you a chance to see if this food upsets your baby's stomach or causes an allergy.

❖ start with single foods rather than mixing foods together. For instance, use just peaches rather than mixing peaches and pears. If your baby gets a rash or an upset stomach, you'll know which food caused the problem. You can mix foods your baby has already tasted.

❖ if, after a few tries, your baby doesn't seem to like a new food, wait a week or two and try again. Your baby needs to eat a variety of foods.

❖ offer mixed foods after your baby has tried each of the foods singly. You might mix two kinds of cereals or vegetables.

*Remember to consult your baby's health care provider before making any changes in baby's diet.

 2-5 These tips may make it easier to add new foods to your baby's diet.

Keep feeding your baby cereals. Add strained or pureed fruits and vegetables, one at a time. Wait three to five days between new foods to check for food allergies. This way you can identify a problem food right away.

Breast milk or formula will still be the main part of your baby's diet. You may also start diluting (adding water to) fruit juice for your baby when she's six to eight months old. Limit her to four to eight ounces of juice a day. Start with pear or apple juice. Test each juice for three to five days for allergies. Offer juices in a cup instead of a bottle. Giving juices in a bottle promotes tooth decay. Don't give your baby soft drinks or sweetened fruit-flavored drinks. These are not good for her.

Your job is to introduce your baby to healthful new tastes. She may make strange faces when she tries a new food. Its taste or texture may surprise her. Her expression may not mean she doesn't like the taste. Offer a food many times. As she gets used to it, she may enjoy it. When she can eat several foods, offer her a variety of tastes at each meal. This will keep mealtime interesting.

Eight to Ten Months

At 8 to 10 months, you can keep using cereals and baby foods. Your baby is also ready to start eating a few finger foods. Babies love to feel the food and feed themselves. Almost any soft, mashed food can be a finger food. You might mash fresh fruits or vegetables for your baby to pick up with her fingers.

At this age, you can also start your baby on strained meats, poultry, and fish. These foods are high in protein. Offer her whole-grain or enriched bread products, such as crackers, hard biscuits, a flour tortilla, or half a bagel. See Figure 2-6 for a sample meal pattern for an eight-month-old.

At about nine months of age, your baby can start to practice using a spoon herself. Use foods that stick to the spoon, such as yogurt, applesauce, mashed potatoes, and infant cereals. Give your baby one spoon and use another yourself to feed her. This will help her practice, while you can make sure she gets enough to eat. It may prevent her from grabbing a spoonful of food out of your hand.

Typical Meal Pattern for 8-Month-Olds

- ❖ Breakfast—iron-fortified infant cereal; fruit, and formula/breast milk
- ❖ Snack—juice/water and toast/finger food.
- ❖ Lunch—meat, vegetable, and formula/breast milk.
- ❖ Snack—juice/water and cracker/finger food.
- ❖ Supper—iron-fortified infant cereal, fruit, and formula/breast milk.
- ❖ Before bedtime—formula/breast milk.

2-6   At eight months old, your baby's meal pattern may look something like this. As long as you follow her health care provider's advice, it's okay if her meal pattern looks a little different.

Your baby should also start eating soft table foods. You can give him lumpier, lightly seasoned foods from the family meal. He will like to grasp pieces of food from his high chair tray and put them in his mouth. Small, tender pieces of macaroni, potatoes, pears, peaches, or tender meat are good choices.

Ten to Twelve Months

When your baby is 10 to 12 months old, you can stop using baby foods. Feed your baby from the family table. Offer her such new foods as egg yolks, chopped fruits and vegetables, and finely chopped meats.

Around the first birthday, your baby will develop good use of a spoon. She can also drink well from a cup. At this age, you can switch from formula to whole milk. You may want to make the switch slowly. Feed her a mixture of formula and whole milk for a few weeks. Then start giving her just whole milk. Remember, your baby needs the fat of whole milk for growth until she is two years old. Don't use lowfat, reduced fat, or fat free milk. See Figure 2-7 for a sample meal pattern for a 12-month-old.

Typical Meal Pattern for 12-Month-Olds

❖ Breakfast-iron—fortified infant cereal, fruit, milk, and toast.

❖ Snack—juice/water and cracker/finger food.

❖ Lunch—meat or cheese, vegetable, fruit, and milk.

❖ Snack—milk/juice and bagel/finger food.

❖ Supper—meat or egg, two vegetables, fruit, and milk.

❖ Before bedtime—juice/milk/water.

2-7 At twelve months old, your baby's meal pattern may look something like this. Of course, your baby's pattern may differ from this somewhat.

Selecting and Preparing Baby Foods

You will probably start using baby foods by the time your baby is six to eight months of age. Your baby needs foods that are very soft and smooth. Packaged baby food from the grocery store is one option. You can also make your own baby food.

Using Packaged Baby Foods

When buying packaged baby foods, read the labels. Check the ingredients listed on the jar. Ingredients are listed in order of the amount. The first three items listed make up most of the food. A food that lists water first is mostly water and may not be very nutritious.

Packaged baby foods often cost more than homemade baby foods. You can save money by comparing labels for best buys. The following are some tips to follow:

- ☛ Boxes of plain baby cereal are a better buy than boxes of cereal with fruit added.
- ☛ Plain fruits have more vitamins than fruit desserts.
- ☛ Plain meats are better buys than mixed dinners.
- ☛ A jar labeled beef and vegetables has more meat than one labeled vegetables and beef.

Be sure the safety button on the top of the jar pops when you open it. This tells you the seal on the jar is locked. No one has tampered with the jar.

To keep prepared baby food safe, don't feed your baby straight from the jar. Saliva from the spoon can spoil the food in the jar. Put a small amount of food into a bowl instead. Throw out any food left in the bowl after your baby has finished. Refrigerate the opened jar and use it within two to three days. Store dry baby cereals in tight containers in the cupboard.

Making Your Own Baby Food

It often costs less to make your own baby food than to use prepared baby foods. This way your baby can also get used to the foods the rest of your family eats. You can puree, mash, or grind table foods for your baby. To do this you can use a fork, potato masher, blender, baby food grinder, or strainer.

Foods that are boiled, steamed, roasted, broiled, or cooked in a microwave can be used to make baby food. Do not add fat, salt, or sugar. Remove fat, bones, and skin from meat. Peel vegetables and fruits. Remove seeds. Add a little liquid if needed to make the food smooth enough. Cooking water, juice, formula, or breast milk may be used.

Avoid using regular canned foods to feed your baby. Too much salt, artificial color, and preservatives have been added. These are not good for your baby.

Be sure to use clean equipment and hands when fixing baby foods. Wash your hands and equipment in hot, soapy water. Rinse and air-dry. Use a plastic cutting board. Plastic cutting boards harbor fewer germs than wooden ones. Plastic cutting boards are also easier to keep clean.

Just like opened jar food, homemade baby food can make your baby sick if it is left at room temperature for more than two hours. Food stored in the refrigerator should be tightly covered. Mashed, raw fruits can be refrigerated for two days. Cooked fruits and vegetables can be kept up to three days. Cooked meats or foods with meat in them should be kept only one to two days.

Foods to Avoid

As a baby and toddler, your young child can choke on food. Some foods slip into children's throats. For this reason, avoid giving your baby or toddler any foods that are small, round, hard, or slippery. Also avoid the following foods, which are major choking hazards for young children:

- ☛ peanuts and seeds
- ☛ raisins
- ☛ whole grapes

- popcorn
- whole, raw carrots (for infants, serve cooked and diced; for toddlers, serve cooked or raw carrot sticks)
- hard candies
- corn chips
- hot dogs (unless sliced lengthwise and then across)
- coarse-textured, crumbly foods, such as cookies
- spoonfuls of peanut butter
- large pieces of tough meat
- olives with pits
- raw cherries with pits

If your child should happen to choke while eating, you should know how to help her. See Figure 2-8 for first aid procedures for a baby who is choking. (See Chapter 7 for the procedures for a choking toddler.) Since choking is common among young children,

What to Do If Your Baby Is Choking

If your baby is choking, help her try to cough the object out. If this doesn't work, use the following first aid steps.

1. **Back slaps**. Lay your baby facedown on your forearm with her head low. Support her head and neck with one hand. Give five sharp slaps between the shoulder blades with the heel of your other hand.

2. **Chest pushes**. If your baby continues choking, turn him over so he faces up. Hold him in your other arm, supporting his back and head. Keep his head below his trunk. Put two fingertips in the center of his chest just below the nipples. Using these two fingers, press downward quickly five times with force.

3. **Check the mouth**. Put your finger in her mouth. If you can see the object, try to hook it out with your finger. Do not put your finger down your child's throat.

4. **Call for help**. If your child is still choking, call 911. Repeat steps 1 and 2 until the paramedics arrive.

2-8 If your infant is choking, a quick response is needed. Knowing the proper first aid techniques can safe her life.

it would be a good idea for you to take an infant/child CPR class. This may be offered through your local hospital, Red Cross, or community center. Learning CPR could help you save your child's life or the life of someone else.

You should also avoid giving your baby honey or corn syrup. These foods can carry botulism spores (a type of bacteria). The spores can make infants very sick. After one year of age, children have a stronger immune system that can protect them from these spores.

Eggs that are uncooked or undercooked are dangerous, too. They can cause a serious infection. Unpasteurized (raw) milk can, too. At 12 months of age, your baby still needs lots of breast milk or formula—2 cups to 3 cups daily. Don't give her cow's milk before she is at least a year old. Cow's milk can cause allergies. Breast milk and formula are easier for her to digest. They are also less likely to cause allergies.

Never give your baby any drinks containing alcohol. Also, avoid giving her soft drinks or drinks with added sugar or artificial sweeteners. Sweet drinks will damage her teeth. They may also encourage her to develop a desire for sweets and sugars.

Clues Your Baby Has Eaten Enough

When your baby is full, he will let you know. Some parents overfeed because they miss their baby's signals. Clues that your baby has eaten enough change as he grows.

Your one- to three-month-old may do the following to show you he has had enough to eat:

- fall asleep
- pull his head away from the nipple
- close his lips tightly
- bite the nipple
- smile
- let go of the nipple

When your baby is four to six months old, he may use these same signs. He will probably add some new ones, though. These include the following:

- ☛ crying or fussing
- ☛ covering his mouth with his hand
- ☛ turning his head away from the spoon

At seven to nine months of age, your baby uses even more clues to let you know he has had enough food. His new clues include the following:

- ☛ keeping his mouth tightly shut
- ☛ playing with his cup, bottle, or spoon
- ☛ throwing his cup, bottle, or spoon
- ☛ waving his hands about wildly

Weaning

Weaning means helping your baby switch from the breast or bottle to a cup for feedings. This is a gradual process that occurs between six months and one year of age. If you wait too long, weaning will be harder. Weaning usually takes a number of weeks.

At six to eight months, your baby will need less formula or breast milk. She will be getting more of her nutrients and calories from solid foods. You can begin to offer juice, breast milk, or formula from a cup. Babies like to drink from a cup even if it is messy. Give your baby a small plastic cup with two handles to hold. See Figure 2-9. These double handles give her an easy grip. Cups with lids and sipper spouts cut down on spills.

Lunchtime or late afternoon feedings are probably the best times for your baby to start using a cup. She will be more likely to eat solid foods at these feedings.

Billie Hainsey

2-9 A sippy cup with handles is easy for baby to hold. At first, expect the baby to play with the cup and spill when drinking.

The following are hints for weaning your baby from the breast or bottle:

☞ Choose a good time to start weaning. Don't start when your baby is sick or upset.

☞ Be sure others who care for your baby know your plan for weaning.

☞ Be consistent once you begin. Don't give in to your baby on a bad day.

☞ Gradually reduce the number of times your baby drinks from the breast or bottle each day. Replace one feeding with breast milk or formula from a cup. Once your baby is familiar with this feeding, use the cup at a second feeding.

☞ Give your baby more attention than usual. She may have a hard time giving up the bottle. Offer her a drink from a cup when she is fussy.

Self-Feeding

Feeding himself is a huge step in your baby's development. Encourage all his attempts to self-feed. Practice will greatly improve his hand-eye coordination. As he reaches for food, grasps it, and puts it in his mouth, your baby develops his small motor skills and balance.

Your baby will begin to look forward to mealtimes. He sees them as playtime as well as a time to eat. Food becomes a plaything, and feeding is messier. Your baby will smear food all over his high chair and himself. Some food will land on the floor. You can put newspapers on the floor to make clean up easier. Keeping the high chair away from the walls will help, too.

Always watch your baby when he is eating. Most babies gag on food at some time. The taste or texture of a new food may make him gag out of surprise. If he does gag, react quickly but calmly.

Gently pat him on the back and encourage him to cough until the food comes out. Comfort your baby and rub his back. With practice, he will become more skilled at eating.

Learning Your Baby's Sleep Patterns

Many experts believe your baby's sleep pattern is set within the first few months. If your baby sleeps a lot during the first year, she will probably continue to sleep a lot. Within the first four months, your baby may start sleeping through the night. Some babies don't do this until much later. They may first start sleeping through the night at 18 months or older. Once your baby starts crawling, she may sleep longer. Crawling will use much of her energy.

Changing Sleep Patterns

Your baby's sleeping patterns will change as he grows older. As a newborn, he will sleep in five or six naps that continue round-the-clock. These naps provide 16 to 20 hours of sleep in a 24-hour period. He will wake up mainly to eat; he needs to be fed often.

Once he starts sleeping through the night, his daytime naps will grow shorter. He will start to stay awake longer during the day. By age one year, your baby might only take two naps—one in the morning and one in the afternoon.

Bedtime Routines

As your baby gets older, you should develop a bedtime routine. This is a set of activities you use in the same way every night to prepare your baby for bed. A bedtime routine is the best way to help her go to sleep. Starting a bedtime routine now will help even more as your baby becomes a toddler. See Figure 2-10 for a list of activities you might include in a bedtime routine.

Bedtime Routine Ideas

- ✤ putting toys away
- ✤ taking a bath
- ✤ brushing teeth
- ✤ singing a good-night song
- ✤ rocking together in a rocking chair
- ✤ reading a story
- ✤ talking about the day's events
- ✤ tucking her in
- ✤ good-night kisses and hugs

2-10 Build a bedtime routine that is meaningful for you and your baby. This will help your baby go to sleep, and it will be a fond memory for both of you.

In your bedtime routine, do everything you can to calm and relax her before sleep. Avoid active play or roughhousing. This kind of play is better for earlier in the day. At the end of your routine, make the room dark, but not so dark she can't see. Your baby needs to realize that night is different from day.

Your baby may become attached to one item that comforts her. This may be a doll, blanket, or favorite soft toy. Don't take this from her. You might use this item in your routine. For instance, you could kiss Dolly when you kiss your baby.

Your baby may rock, suck her thumb, rub her ears, or twist her hair as she prepares to go to sleep. Don't try to change this behavior. It is part of her bedtime routine. These habits help her feel secure. She will give them up when she is ready.

Having a simple routine helps most children learn to sleep through the night. The key is to be consistent. Use the same routine in the same order every night. This way your child knows what to expect. Try to put your baby to sleep at about the same time every night.

A bedtime routine will not work with every infant, though. Some babies require an extra amount of patience. Only growing older will allow these babies to sleep through the night. If your baby is clingy and sleepless at night, stay with him for a while. Hold him close, rock him, soothe him, and sing softly to him. Hold your baby and walk with him until he feels secure. This should take only a few minutes.

Try the following if your baby awakens during the night:

- ☞ Make sure he is not too hot nor too cold.
- ☞ Check his diaper.
- ☞ Don't keep checking to see if your baby is asleep.
- ☞ If your baby suddenly becomes sleepless, think about what may be causing it. Has there been a change in routine?
- ☞ Give your baby something to play with in bed, such as a favorite soft toy or book.

Sudden Infant Death Syndrome (SIDS)

Sudden infant death syndrome (SIDS) is the unexpected death of a baby who seems healthy. The baby stops breathing for no clear reason, usually during the night. SIDS is a major cause of infant death. It occurs in about two of every thousand babies. SIDS happens most often in babies under six months old.

SIDS is not caused by anything parents do or fail to do. Research does suggest some simple ways to protect your baby from SIDS. The following tips can also help him breathe more easily:

- ☞ Put your baby to sleep on his <u>back</u> or <u>side</u> instead of his stomach.
- ☞ Make sure your baby sleeps on a firm mattress rather than a soft mattress or waterbed.
- ☞ Keep your baby from sleeping face down on soft or heavy bedding. Consider using a blanket sleeper rather than heavy blankets.
- ☞ Be sure your baby isn't wrapped too warmly in clothing and blankets. You don't want him to get too hot.
- ☞ If you smoke, quit. Keep your baby away from smoke.

Meeting Your Baby's Clothing Needs

Your baby is growing rapidly. She quickly outgrows her clothes. Comfortable, safe, and practical clothing is a must. You don't have to spend lots of money on your baby's clothes, though. Family and friends may loan you some clothes their children have outgrown. Garage sales and secondhand stores are also good sources of used children's clothing.

Comfortable

Look for clothing that is soft and comfortable. Avoid stitching, seams, and fabrics that are rough or stiff. Cotton fabrics are a good choice. These feel soft on your baby's skin. See Figure 2-11. Choose clothes that will give him the most comfort and warmth. Pay special attention to fastenings at the cuffs, ankles, and neck. Be sure these won't cause him discomfort.

Your baby's clothing must allow him to move easily. Avoid tight clothing. Buy clothing a size or two larger. This lets him move more freely. It will also last longer because your baby won't outgrow it as fast. Clothing that is much too big is a hazard, though. It can cause your baby to become tangled and choke.

Safe

Your baby's safety is a big concern. By law, children's sleepwear must be <u>flame retardant</u>. This means it has been treated with chemicals that keep it from catching on fire easily. Make sure the sleepwear you buy for your baby is flame retardant. You can look for this information on the labels before buying. Check the label for washing instructions, too. Avoid using fabric softener in the

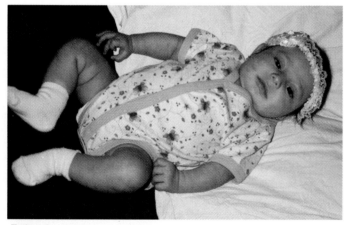

Esther Jacome

 Cotton clothing keeps this baby comfortable. The snaps at the crotch allow for easy diaper changes.

washer or dryer with your baby's sleepwear. The chemicals in these softeners can interfere with the chemicals in the clothing that protect your baby against fire.

Fasteners are also a safety concern. Gripper snaps and lightweight zippers are best. Avoid buttons or trims that might come off easily. These can be swallowed or cause choking. Trims should be soft and safe. You will also want to avoid buying clothing with drawstrings that could strangle your baby. If your baby already has some clothing with drawstrings, remove the drawstrings to make the clothing safer.

Practical

You will want to buy clothing that is practical, or easy to use and care for. Choose clothing you can wash by machine. Your baby's clothes must be washed often. She will spit up and drool. Her diapers may leak, and accidents will happen. Clothes that must be washed by hand take more work from you. Frequent dry-cleaning can be costly.

Ease of dressing is also important. Choose clothing that makes dressing more comfortable for your baby and easier for you. Check the fastenings. Clothes that snap at the crotch seam allow easy access to the diaper area. Without these snaps, the garment must be taken off for each diaper change. Clothes that snap at the neckline allow an item to be worn longer. Without these snaps, the garment must be pulled over your baby's head. As her head grows, she will quickly outgrow this type of garment. Choose clothes that fasten down the front rather than down the back. Front-fastening clothes let you dress your baby without having to turn her over. See Figure 2-12 for more tips on choosing practical clothing.

Tips for Choosing Practical Clothing

❖ White clothing gets soiled and stained easily. It starts to look dingy after several washings. Choose colored clothing for everyday wear.

❖ All-in-one suits with snap fastenings are ideal for keeping baby warm.

❖ Babies lose socks and booties very easily. For girls, tights are practical as well as warm. For boys, footed clothing may work well.

❖ Two-piece sweat suits are warm and comfortable. These can be worn longer than some one-piece outfits, and they allow for growth.

❖ Pairing overalls with a T-shirt is comfortable. Choose overalls with snap openings at the crotch for easier diaper changes.

❖ Hats can be both practical and cute. For warm weather, choose a hat with ties or elastic and a wide brim for sun protection. Hats with tie-down earflaps keep your baby's head warm in winter.

❖ Be sure your baby's knees are protected when crawling. Look for pants with reinforced knees.

2-12 For everyday wear, infants need practical clothing. This type of clothing is easy to use and care for.

Clothing Sizes

Knowing what size clothes to buy for your baby takes practice. It can be a little confusing. Sizes for baby clothes may be listed in three ways. First, sizes such as <u>small</u>, <u>medium</u>, and <u>large</u> may be used. Second, sizes may be given as an age range, such as <u>newborn</u>, <u>3 to 6 months</u>, or <u>12 months</u>. Third, a weight range, such as <u>6 to 10 pounds</u>, <u>10 to 16 pounds</u>, or <u>18 to 24 pounds</u>, may be given as the size.

Some clothing labels give more than one type of size listing. If you can, select your baby's clothing based on his weight. This tends to be the most accurate. When no weight is given, you can look at the item and estimate whether it would fit your baby. (Be sure the store allows returns in case you guess wrong!) Once you know what size your baby is, you can buy other items in that size. Keep in mind that clothing sizes may vary from one brand to another.

Shoes

Your baby doesn't really need shoes until after she starts walking outside. Most baby shoes are just for style or decoration. Some parents buy a pair of dress shoes for their infants. The babies wear these shoes for pictures, special occasions, or church. This is not necessary, though. You can use footed clothing and socks to keep your baby's feet warm. When she first starts to walk indoors, bare feet are best. Socks or shoes can cause her to slip.

Washing Baby's Clothes

Before washing your baby's clothes, carefully read the care labels. A care label is a small tag sewn into a garment that tells you how to care for it. The care label will tell you whether you should wash the item by hand or in a machine. It will tell you what temperature of water to use, and how to dry the garment. The care label will also tell you which items must be dry-cleaned. (You may want to limit the number of items you buy that must be dry-cleaned. This can be very costly.) Follow the directions. This will make your baby's clothing last longer.

Treat all stains with a stain remover before washing. This keeps food and juice stains from setting. Some stain removers should be used right before you wash the clothes. Others can be applied just after a stain occurs, even if you won't be doing laundry for a few days.

You may wonder whether you can wash your baby's clothes with the same laundry soap the rest of the family uses. The answer is maybe, but it will depend on how sensitive your baby's skin is. You can test one garment or one load of clothes by washing it with your regular laundry soap. If your baby's skin seems to itch or break into a rash, stop using this detergent. Switch to a detergent made just for baby clothes. This kind of detergent has fewer harsh chemicals. It is gentler and milder, so it will be less likely to irritate your baby's skin. Some parents prefer to use a baby detergent even if their baby's skin can tolerate the family's regular soap.

☞ Your baby needs healthful foods to grow and develop. Her body and brain development depends on the foods she eats. Her food needs will change as she grows, and it's your job as her parent to meet these changing food needs.

☞ Ask your baby's health care provider when to start solid foods. For most babies, this is at 4 to 6 months. Try infant rice cereal first. Add other new foods one at a time. If you use packaged baby foods, choose them carefully. If you make baby food, mash or grind table food to make it soft and smooth.

☞ Don't give your baby small, round, or hard foods that might cause him to choke. Also avoid honey, corn syrup, raw eggs, cow's milk, soda, sweet drinks, and alcohol.

☞ By the time your baby is 12 months old, she can eat from the family table. You may be almost done weaning her from the breast or bottle to a cup. She can start drinking whole cow's milk at about the first birthday. Encourage your baby's efforts to feed herself. This is good for her hand-eye coordination, but it will be messy.

☞ Within a few months, your baby takes longer naps and may start to sleep through the night. A simple bedtime routine can help him get to sleep. Protect your baby from sudden infant death syndrome (SIDS) by putting him on his back or side to sleep. Also, keep him away from cigarette smoke.

☞ Your baby outgrows her clothes quickly in the first year. Choose clothing for her that is comfortable, safe, and practical. Check the labels to find the right size. Follow the instructions on the care label when washing your baby's clothes.

Chapter 3
Your Baby's Intellectual, Social, and Emotional Development

As you know, your infant develops at a rapid pace. Her body isn't the only part of her that's growing and changing, though. Intellectual, social, and emotional development start now, too. How she learns, relates to others, and feels about herself depends largely on your influence. As her parent and teacher, it's your job to guide your baby's development. This chapter describes intellectual, social, and emotional development in the first year. It also tells you how to meet your baby's needs in these areas.

Your Baby's Intellectual Development

As you learned in Chapter 1, intellectual development means the growth of the mind and its thinking abilities. This kind of development allows your baby to remember, think, reason, and solve simple problems. He starts to build these skills at birth.

His intellectual development depends, of course, upon the brain. Your baby was born with over 100 billion neurons (brain cells). His brain will double in weight by his first birthday. This weight gain is caused by synapses that are forming. These synapses connect different parts of the brain. Connections form only when your baby's brain is stimulated. New sights, sounds, smells, tastes, and touches make him think. This excites him! See Figure 3-1 for ideas on providing stimulation for your baby's growing brain.

Your baby's first few weeks of life are confusing. His brain must sort out many sights, sounds, and smells. Your face and voice may be the first things he recognizes. He will respond when he sees, hears,

Quick Ways to Stimulate Baby's Brain

It takes less than two minutes to:
* ❖ give your baby a hug and kiss.
* ❖ tickle your baby's tummy.
* ❖ smile at your baby.
* ❖ show your baby two or three pictures in a book.
* ❖ hold your baby up to see pictures on the wall or look out the window.
* ❖ sing a song for your baby.
* ❖ point out a flower or an animal.
* ❖ say, "I love you" to your baby.

 If you have even a couple of minutes, you have time to build your baby's brain power! His brain can be stimulated in many quick and easy ways.

or smells you. He may smile, jerk his arms and legs, coo, or gurgle. This means he recognizes you! It is an intellectual development milestone.

In the next month, your baby becomes more alert. He can focus for short periods. For example, when your baby hears a sound, he will look around. Toys, objects, and pictures become very interesting. Your baby may stare at these—they hold his attention.

As reflex actions fade, your baby can move on his own. Now he must think about how he wants to move. His thought stimulates the muscles to move. Movements, in turn, build the brain even more. In this way, he uses his senses and motor skills to learn about the world around him. This exploration also helps build his intellectual skills.

This makes your baby more aware of his own body. Your baby spends lots of time looking at and moving his hands. Playing with his feet is fun, too! See Figure 3-2. Your baby starts using his body to answer your questions, smiles, and looks. He may reply with smiles, gurgles, waves, and cycling motions.

At about four months, your baby likes to sit up so he can look around. You can prop him up near you against a cushion, or put him in an infant seat. Spending all his time lying down is boring! Your baby wants to see everything.

In the next few months, your baby's attention span grows. He spends more time looking at and touching objects. Your baby makes sounds to get your attention. He may start putting his arms out so you can pick him up.

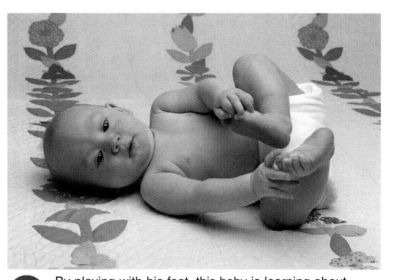

3-2 By playing with his feet, this baby is learning about his body.

At seven to eight months, your baby starts learning the meaning of some words, such as the word <u>no</u>. He can move around more now and wants to explore everything. Your baby is curious about anything within reach. His memory is developing.

A month or two later (9 to 10 months), your baby reaches another important milestone. He develops object permanence. This means he knows an object still exists even if he can't see it. Now, when you hide a toy under a blanket, he remembers it is still there. When he drops something off his high chair tray, he knows where it is. He will want you to pick the object up so he can drop it again! This is a fun game for him. You may not enjoy picking up an object many times in a row. If you keep in mind your baby is learning from this, it may help.

At the end of the first year, your baby's memory is much sharper. He can hunt for a toy and remember where he saw it last. Your baby has favorite people and toys. He begins to anticipate events. Suppose he sees you put on your coat and get your purse. From these cues, baby knows you are leaving. When it is dark outside, he knows it is time for his bath, story, and bed.

You can boost your child's development by giving him plenty of chances to play. Watch your baby's expression as he plays. Many times, you can see he's learning. During this first year, he will reach for a toy, grasp it, and turn it over. He will hold the toy, bang it, and drop it. What a fun way to learn!

Your baby needs plenty of toys to play with and explore. These don't need to be expensive educational toys, though. Simple toys can teach him, too. Even common household objects can serve as playthings. See Figure 3-3.

Developing Language Skills

Your baby was born to talk! Learning language is part of her intellectual development. This slow process goes on every day. Babies follow the same order in learning to talk. (See the Developmental Milestones chart for intellectual development at the end of this chapter.)

At birth, your newborn will react to human voices. She can also sense when you are talking to her. She will react by looking and moving her whole body. Crying is another way she can communicate with you. The second month of life is a peak month for crying. Babies fuss and make unhappy noises when they need something. Respond quickly to your fussy or crying baby. This will teach her she doesn't have to scream to be heard.

Household Items or Baby Toys?

Your baby will enjoy playing with many common household items. Choose items that are safe for the baby to explore. These include the following:

- empty thread spools (be sure they're too big to swallow)
- small, lightweight metal saucepans and lids
- metal baking pans
- plastic cups, containers, and lids
- plastic jars and lids with clothespins, seeds, beads, or other objects inside (be sure the lids can't come off, so your baby won't swallow the objects inside)
- plastic ice cube trays
- strainers, whisks, and other safe kitchen utensils
- plastic bottles of all sizes and shapes

3-3 Parents may be frustrated if their baby passes up expensive toys to play with common household items. Keep in mind he learns from using these objects, too.

Even before she can talk, your baby is learning about language. Listening to you talk also teaches her to tell the difference between speech and other sounds. (This usually happens at about one month of age.) It also stimulates her brain to form connections. When these connections are strong, they will allow your baby to start speaking. Your baby can also learn about pitches, tones, words, and meanings. See Figure 3-4 for tips on talking with your baby.

Your baby will also need to develop more physically before she will be able to talk. A newborn's mouth is very shallow. She can't control her tongue, jaw, and lips, either. Your baby's ability to speak depends upon development in the brain, mouth, and jaw.

At three and four months, babies love to make cooing noises. A coo is a pleasant sound, such as <u>ooh</u> or <u>ah</u>. Babies coo now when others talk with them. The more you react to her sounds, the more sounds she will make. Laugh and giggle a lot when you talk to your baby.

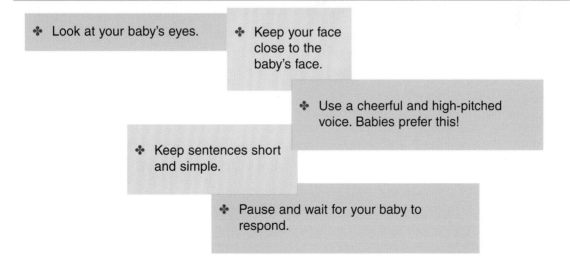

Tips for Talking with Your Baby

When you talk with your baby, remember to do the following:

❖ Look at your baby's eyes.

❖ Keep your face close to the baby's face.

❖ Use a cheerful and high-pitched voice. Babies prefer this!

❖ Keep sentences short and simple.

❖ Pause and wait for your baby to respond.

3-4   By using these tips, you can engage your baby in a conversation. This will hold baby's interest and teach her about communication.

Your baby is learning that part of conversation is taking turns. Your baby "talks" and then waits for you to talk. Then it is baby's turn again.

Try to talk to your baby all the time. For instance, talk to her when you make dinner or give her a bath. As you bathe baby, point to her foot and say foot. Naming games like "Where is baby's hand" are fun. This is a good way for baby to begin to learn that words have meanings.

Babbling develops after cooing, usually at five or six months. Babbling means using, repeating, or stringing together sounds like da, ba, and gi. This is an important step in learning to talk. Babies all over the world babble before they learn to talk. If you listen to your baby's babbling, you can almost hear how she feels. Babies show their feelings by babbling, such as being happy, angry, or excited.

At seven and eight months, your baby is starting to understand the meanings of words. She will know what it means if you say no firmly. Help your baby learn new words. Read books to your baby and show her the pictures. Repeat the names of the things she sees. Speak clearly and slowly. Be a good language model for your child. Nursery rhymes, simple songs, and clapping games are fun for both of you.

At 9 or 10 months, your baby may use a sound like ba to mean many different things. Listen. This is her first try at saying words. Talking is not far away. Between 9 and 12 months, your baby might mix a real word or two in with all this babbling.

By 11 or 12 months, your baby may use one or two words with meaning. Praise your baby for every new word, and repeat the word. Your baby will say this word over and over because she likes your approval. This will help your baby practice her new words.

Your Baby's Social and Emotional Development

In his first year, your baby grows quite a bit both emotionally and socially. He starts as a helpless newborn who can't communicate well. By his first birthday, he'll be expressing his feelings and building relationships.

(To learn more about specific milestones, see the <u>Developmental Milestones</u> chart for social and emotional development at the end of this chapter. This chart lists many developments in these areas during the first year.)

Your baby shows his emotions through the sounds, body movements, and the faces he makes. Watch him carefully. You can learn to read his emotions this way. At just a few weeks old, your baby may show anger, surprise, interest, happiness, sadness, and disgust. In the months to come, he can express even more feelings. Expressing feelings is a big part of his emotional development.

The first year is an important one for social development, too. You are the best person to teach your baby how to love. He's becoming attached to you. This attachment builds the foundation of his future relationships. The way you touch, hold, and nurture your child shapes his emotional skills and well-being. See Figure 3-5.

Your baby also watches you as an example of how to interact with others. It all begins with the relationship you and your baby share. You can learn quite a bit from your baby by watching her and reading her behavior.

Reading Your Baby's Cues

You can help your baby develop socially and emotionally. One way to do this is to read the cues she is giving you. By watching your baby closely, you can learn to read these cues. You can tell many of her emotions by her facial expressions. You can tell when she is happy, angry, hungry, or tired.

Your baby can also tell you she wants to engage (enter play and share with you). When she looks into your face, she is ready to engage. Your baby may break off

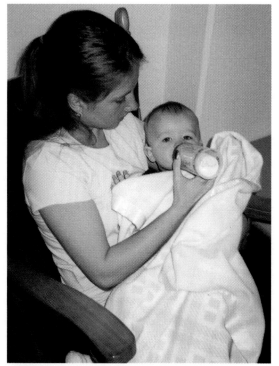

 Holding your baby during feedings shows he matters to you. Feeling secure and loved boosts your baby's brain growth.

the gaze first—maybe for only a second—and then look back into your face again. This is a sign she wants to engage. When she is quiet and alert, this is a good time to engage.

Other signs your baby wants to share with you are cooing and having open, relaxed hands and shoulders. She may pedal her feet and then stop. This is a signal that it's your turn to join the "conversation." When your baby wants to engage, you can spend time interacting with her. This boosts her development.

Also important is knowing when your baby doesn't want to play. At these times, you can avoid play or introduce new activities. When your baby wants to stop or avoid play, this means she wants to disengage. This may mean she is getting too excited and needs a little break. It is <u>not</u> a sign she is rejecting you.

Your baby will give you clues when she wants to disengage. These include turning her eyes away, shutting her eyes tight, blinking, or yawning. Other ways are sneezing, hiccuping, increased sucking noises, whimpering, and crying. Older babies use more adultlike cues when they want to disengage. These include lowering the head, crawling away, pushing you away, clenching their mouths shut, or saying <u>no</u>.

When your baby shows these signs, it means she needs a different kind of attention. Try using the suggestions in Figure 3-6 to soothe her.

Identifying Your Baby's Temperament

Your baby's personality starts to show during infancy. His typical response to his surroundings is called his temperament. One baby might be cheerful and cooperative most of the time. This is part of his temperament. Another baby might be sensitive, withdrawn, and fussy. This is part of his temperament. It influences how he reacts to the world.

Ways to Soothe Your Baby

✤ Provide quiet, steady sounds, such as a fan, dryer, vacuum, soft music, or recorded human heartbeat. These can soothe your baby.

✤ Cuddle him for a while. Gently rock, hold, touch, and pat him.

✤ Use a soft light in your baby's room. Keep the room a little warmer to help make her sleepy.

✤ Wrap your baby snugly in a soft blanket. This will help him feel warm and secure.

✤ Provide smooth, gentle motion for your baby. Rock her, carry her, or take her for a ride in a stroller or car. Be sure to use a car seat for any car ride.

3-6 When your baby wants to disengage, you can use these tips to soothe her. This is the type of attention she needs when she's overly excited.

Research shows most children can be placed into one of three temperament patterns. These are easy, slow to warm up, and difficult. Over two-thirds of all babies fit into one of these patterns. (Some babies are in more than one group, while others don't fit any of these patterns.)

Easy

As its name suggests, children in this group have easy-going temperaments. They often eat, sleep, and have bowel movements in a regular pattern. These children are usually active, cheerful, and happy. They adapt quickly and have mild responses to change.

A child with an easy temperament doesn't spend much time crying. She likes to watch, listen to, and play with people and objects. This child smiles, coos, and babbles at people she doesn't

Almost half of all babies have an easy temperament. They adjust to change easily and are usually happy.

even know. About forty percent of all children have an easy temperament. See Figure 3-7.

Slow to Warm Up

Almost ten percent of children are slow to warm up. It takes them time to try new things. These children are less active and pull back from new experiences. They adapt slowly to change and have mild emotional reactions.

A child who warms up slowly needs plenty of time to adjust to changes. She often hesitates in new situations. This child likes to watch for a time before entering an activity or going to a new person. Once she feels comfortable, though, she will join right in.

If your baby is slow to warm up, give her plenty of time. Warn your baby of changes that are coming. Don't rush her or be impatient. Reassure her this new activity or person is okay. Wait for her to feel comfortable. Be sure to give her plenty of attention. Outgoing or demanding babies are louder, so they usually get attention first. Babies who warm up slowly may be ignored or overlooked by others.

Difficult

The third temperament style is called difficult. It gets its name because it is a harder style for parents to work with. About ten percent of children are in this group. A child with this temperament usually eats, sleeps, and has bowel movements on an irregular basis. This child is very sensitive and reacts negatively to change. She pulls away from new situations and does not adapt well.

A baby with a difficult temperament may spend a lot of time crying. She becomes tense and has trouble paying attention to people or things. If your baby has this temperament, keep in mind she's not being difficult on purpose. Your baby is not bad. She was born with this response style, and it may change as she gets older. Your baby just needs more care and patience than other babies. Respond quickly to her cries. Remember it's not your baby but her <u>style</u> that can be hard to handle. The more positively you respond, the better it is for her.

Attachment

Attachment is a strong emotional tie people feel toward special people in their lives. Babies become attached to familiar people who meet their needs. Your baby will become emotionally attached to you during his first year of life. See Figure 3-8. You feel attached to your baby, too. This sense of attachment includes your love and concern for him. Your baby may also form attachments to other people and a favorite stuffed toy or blanket.

Olaya Grado, GRADS student at Artesia High School

 Your newborn will gaze at you as you hold him in your arms.

Attachment is the result of a process called bonding. Bonding is the formation of a close personal relationship. This process starts at birth. Your baby shows signs of pleasure when you appear. He smiles, wiggles, and gurgles when he sees you. In turn, you comfort, hold, and nurture your newborn. When you promptly meet your baby's needs for food and sensitive care, he learns he can count on you. A sense of trust develops. He comes to see the world as a comforting, not scary, place. You and your baby are forming a strong bond.

Attachment builds gradually during the first year. From birth to six weeks, your baby is just getting to know you. Your baby learns your voice and scent. When he cries, smiles, grasps your hand, and gazes into your eyes, it brings the two of you closer. At this age, though, he won't be frantic if you leave for a short time. It doesn't bother him if someone else cares for him while you're gone.

Starting at about six weeks, attachment begins to grow. At this time, your baby can tell the difference between familiar people and strangers. His actions reflect this. With you, he will make sounds and play. He may not use these same skills with strangers. Your baby notices his actions affect your behavior toward him. A sense of trust starts to form. Your baby knows you will respond to his cues. At this age, he can tell a familiar person from a stranger. He still doesn't cry or make a big fuss when left with an unfamiliar person, though.

In the last half of the first year, your baby grows even more attached. This starts at six to eight months, and it may last through the second year. By now, your baby is very attached to you. He prefers you over everyone else and is upset when you leave him. Your baby shows this separation anxiety by crying, fussing, clinging, protesting, and being very unhappy!

Separation anxiety often starts at about eight months. This anxiety slowly builds. It peaks at about 15 months and then slowly starts to fade. See Figure 3-9. By about two years of age, it's usually gone.

As a parent, you may find it hard to handle this anxiety. Your baby may cling to you, cry, and scream. This may make you just as upset as he is. If your baby reacts strongly to your leaving, you may be tempted to avoid this scene altogether. It might seem easier to sneak out of the room so your baby won't see you leave. You might try to distract him with a special toy and step out when he's not looking.

3-9 As a young toddler, your child may feel separation anxiety most strongly. When you leave her, comfort her and reassure her you will return.

Doing these things may make you feel better about leaving, but they don't help your baby. In fact, they make it even more stressful for him. Imagine your baby turning around to find his parent has disappeared! He might feel scared, tense, or even abandoned. These feelings can destroy the sense of trust you are working to build. They can make your baby feel insecure. He may wonder if you'll return.

It is better to tell your baby you're leaving and will be back soon. Tell him you love him, and give him a hug or kiss. Use the same good-bye routine each time you leave. This will help him feel secure. He can think ahead to what will happen next. He will soon learn you always come back for him.

Separation anxiety is a normal part of growing up. It means your baby is developing a close relationship with you. In the meantime, try not to be too upset about your baby's reaction. Most infants and toddlers cry for a few minutes when their parents leave. If they're in good care, these babies soon settle down and feel better.

Need for Love and Attention

To grow up happy and healthy, babies need love and attention. This is just as vital to growth as food. Without love and attention, babies can develop failure to thrive. This physical growth disorder can occur even when a baby's basic physical needs are met. Children with this condition don't grow to their full size—they remain smaller. They may also have various learning and emotional problems.

Give your child plenty of love, attention, and stimulation. This will keep him happy and healthy. It will meet his social and emotional needs and help his brain grow.

Your Baby Wants to Be Part of the Family

Your baby feels a social need to belong. See Figure 3-10. He likes being a member of the family with all its routines and rules. Include your baby in family activities as soon as possible. Take him shopping, on outings, and visiting loved ones as early as possible. He needs to learn how to fit in with others.

Talk to your baby about new people he sees. His memory is very short. At this age, he won't remember a person he sees once a week or less. This kind of memory develops a few months later.

 3-10 This baby likes to feel he's part of the family. He enjoys the company of his older cousin, who lives in the same house with him.

Your baby learns by watching you interact with family members and friends. Teach him about family relationships. He will copy what he sees you do. You are his most important role model.

☛ Your baby's intellectual development starts at birth. Her brain is growing rapidly. Your baby will use her senses and muscles to explore and learn about the world. She will learn that an object still exists even if she can't see it.

☛ Before your baby can talk, he must grow more physically. His brain must also be ready to learn language. He will start to make a variety of sounds that lead to language. By his first birthday, your baby will likely say at least one word with meaning.

☛ Your baby's first year is one of rapid social and emotional growth. By the end of this year, your baby starts to learn she's a separate person from you. She seeks approval, shows affection, and likes to communicate.

☞ It's important to read your baby's cues. This helps you give him the kind of attention he needs. When your baby is quiet and alert, he may want to engage. He will let you know when he is ready to disengage.

☞ Your baby's temperament is her typical response to her world. Most babies have one of three temperament patterns: easy, slow-to-warm-up, or difficult. Some babies have more than one style.

☞ Attachment develops in the first year. It results from the bonding between parents and baby. Your baby is developing a special relationship with you. This relationship will set the tone for his future relationships.

☞ Your baby needs your love and attention. This helps her grow healthy and strong. She also has a strong social need to belong. She enjoys being with her family members. Your baby watches how you interact with others. You are her role model.

Birth to 12 Months

As your newborn, I
- react to people's voices.
- communicate by crying.
- become quiet when you pick me up.
- stop sucking to listen or look at something.

As your one-month-old, I
- stay awake and alert about one hour in ten.
- remember an object if it reappears within a second or two.
- cry for assistance.
- start vocalizing.
- try to make cooing sounds.

As your two-month-old, I
- can follow a moving object with my eyes.
- recognize my favorite things, like a rattle or toy.
- can look to where you're looking and follow your gaze.
- get excited when I know mealtime is coming.
- study my own hand movements.
- notice differences in faces, voices, tastes, and objects.

As your three-month-old, I
- begin to show memory. I can wait for my food a little longer when I know it's coming.
- cry less than before.
- use information I gather from all my senses.
- explore my own face, eyes, and mouth by using my hands.
- can tell the difference between speech and other sounds.
- turn my head toward a voice I hear.

As your four-month-old, I
- have responsive periods that last as long as an hour.
- make simple vowel sounds like *ooh* and *ah*.
- remember important people overnight or longer.
- can tell by looking whether a toy is near or far.
- like some toys better than others. I have favorites.
- remember simple daily routines. For instance, seeing my bottle may remind me that I get to eat next.
- make several sounds and imitate tones of voice you use.

As your five-month-old, I
- babble to myself, my toys, other objects, and people.
- utter vowel sounds and use consonants such as *b*, *d*, *l*, and *m*.
- may lean over to look for a fallen toy.
- deliberately imitate your sounds and movements.
- recognize familiar people by their voices.
- turn objects and toys over to get another view.

As your six-month-old, I
- inspect objects for a long time.
- may compare two objects I am holding.
- start to understand some words by your tone of voice.
- am beginning to make sounds such as *f*, *sh*, *th*, *m* and *n*.
- recognize my name when I hear it.
- enjoy playing copycat games like clapping and imitating the sounds I hear.

(Continued)

Developmental Milestones: Intellectual Development

Birth to 12 Months

As your seven-month-old, I

❖ make sounds like *mama* and *dada*, but I don't know what they mean yet.

❖ use a special sound to get your attention.

❖ try to imitate the sounds I hear.

❖ begin to learn about cause and effect. This means I learn when one event happens, it can cause something else to occur.

❖ enjoy noisy toys.

❖ understand the meaning of *no* by the tone of your voice.

❖ remember events that just happened.

As your eight-month-old, I

❖ spend lots of time examining objects with my eyes and hands.

❖ can tell if people are happy or angry by their looks and voice.

❖ solve simple problems like how to take something apart.

❖ mimic people's sounds and jaw movements.

❖ can recall past events.

As your nine-month-old, I

❖ pay close attention to adults talking.

❖ start to add *t* and *w* to speech sounds.

❖ can uncover a toy after I watch you hide it under a blanket.

❖ remember a game, toy, or person from yesterday.

❖ may wave good-bye.

❖ become afraid of heights as I learn about vertical distance.

❖ follow very simple directions like "Come here" and "Give it to me".

As your ten-month-old, I

❖ connect the words *mama* and *dada* to my parents.

❖ imitate your actions more than before

❖ may repeat the same sound over and over again.

❖ open drawers and cabinets to see what's inside.

❖ get upset if a toy is taken away.

❖ enjoy playing simple games like peek-a-boo.

❖ try to figure things out by myself.

As your eleven-month-old, I

❖ like to practice fitting things together.

❖ answer to my own name.

❖ jabber with feeling.

❖ say my first word or maybe a few words, such as *mama*, *dada*, and *no*.

❖ point to objects I want and grunt.

❖ mix real words in with my babbling.

❖ can understand simple questions like "Where is the ball?"

As your twelve-month-old, I

❖ play hiding games with my toys.

❖ like to stack blocks, put cups inside each other, and drop objects into containers.

❖ enjoy looking at pictures in books.

❖ can identify some body parts and animals.

❖ remember events for longer periods.

❖ copy the behaviors, sounds, and words you use.

71

Birth to 12 Months

As your newborn, I

❖ respond to your smell, touch, voice, and face.

❖ am learning to recognize you.

❖ cry to communicate with you.

❖ stop crying when you pick me up.

❖ like to be held close to you.

❖ can show excitement and distress.

As your one-month-old, I

❖ am comforted by a human face.

❖ know your voice.

❖ can make eye contact with you.

❖ use body, mouth, and tongue movements to get your attention.

❖ want to be close to you.

❖ adjust my position to the body of the person who is holding me.

❖ recognize and respond to you, my parent.

As your two-month-old, I

❖ can smile at you.

❖ quiet myself by sucking. I may like to use a pacifier or my hands and fingers.

❖ respond with excitement when I see you.

❖ stay awake longer if you play with me.

❖ show affection by kicking, waving arms, smiling.

❖ feel happy, sad, or uncomfortable at times.

❖ need lots of cuddling and holding.

❖ fuss when I'm unhappy.

As your three-month-old, I

❖ can sense your emotions.

❖ feel secure when you hold me close.

❖ begin to recognize and tell the differences among family members.

❖ smile easily on my own, without seeing someone else do it first.

❖ cry less now.

❖ coo, make faces, and gurgle in response to sounds.

❖ use my sounds to tell you how I feel and what I need.

As your four-month-old, I

❖ make a noise or wiggle to catch your attention when you're nearby.

❖ show delight with a laugh, squeal, or chuckle.

❖ have a favorite toy or special object. I may cry if you interrupt my play.

❖ turn to the sound of your voice and wiggle with pleasure when I see you.

❖ want to sit or be propped up so I can watch you.

❖ dislike being left alone.

❖ like to see myself in the mirror. I may even smile at my image.

❖ try to soothe myself when I'm tired or upset.

❖ may stop eating to play.

(Continued)

As your five-month-old, I

✤ smile and make sounds to get your attention.

✤ protest and resist if you try to take my toy away.

✤ can tell a familiar face from a stranger.

✤ may start to resent strangers a little now.

✤ know my family members and may smile at familiar people.

✤ like to be around other infants and children.

As your six-month-old, I

✤ become demanding when my cries are not answered.

✤ stop crying when you talk to me.

✤ know the difference between an angry voice and a friendly voice.

✤ may have sudden mood changes.

✤ vocalize to express my feelings.

✤ am bothered by strangers and may cling to you when they're around.

✤ enjoy hugs, kisses, and pats.

✤ respond to music by humming, cooing, or moving my body.

As your seven-month-old, I

✤ am playful.

✤ am developing a sense of humor and like to tease.

✤ start to resist doing things I don't want to do.

✤ express interest in interacting with others.

✤ prefer you over other people.

✤ want you to hold me when strangers are around.

As your eight-month-old, I

✤ push away any objects I don't want.

✤ pat, smile at, and try to kiss my image in the mirror.

✤ shout for attention.

✤ imitate people some time after I have seen them.

✤ enjoy being with older children.

✤ show some independence; want to explore new places with you nearby.

✤ get frustrated or lose my temper when I can't find something.

✤ am attached to you and afraid of strangers. I feel unhappy when you leave me for even a short time.

As your nine-month-old, I

✤ want to play by myself but near you.

✤ initiate play with you and others.

✤ like to show off.

✤ enjoy water play.

✤ give you kisses and hugs to show my love. I may also wave bye-bye.

✤ grunt, shriek, and babble to communicate with you.

✤ may start to fear things that didn't scare me before, such as heights, taking a bath, or hearing a vacuum cleaner.

✤ am very sensitive. I may cry if I see another baby cry.

(Continued)

Birth to 12 Months

As your ten-month-old, I

✤ am more aware of myself and seek your approval more often.

✤ want companionship and attention.

✤ enjoy playing social games like pat-a-cake and peek-a-boo.

✤ hug, pat, and show love to my favorite stuffed toy.

✤ become very determined when I'm doing a task.

✤ show my moods with my facial expression and body posture.

As your eleven-month-old, I

✤ am beginning to realize I'm a person separate from you.

✤ enjoy rolling a ball back and forth with you.

✤ don't always want to cooperate.

✤ show feelings of guilt when I do something wrong.

✤ imitate the gestures, expressions, and sounds others make.

✤ work to avoid your disapproval of me.

✤ like to practice communicating with adults.

✤ understand that *no* means *stop doing that*. I still can't always make myself stop what I am doing unless you redirect my attention to something else.

As your twelve-month-old, I

✤ protest strongly when you stop my play. I may show anger if you take my toy away.

✤ may start throwing tantrums when I don't get my way.

✤ sometimes resist taking a nap.

✤ like to join in family activities, such as eating meals with the family.

✤ feel relieved when you return from being away.

✤ might refuse to eat my meal or try new foods.

✤ show my sense of humor more often now.

✤ use pretend play as I feed, cuddle, and bathe my favorite toy or doll.

Chapter 4 Keeping Your Baby Healthy and Safe

It's your job to keep your baby healthy and safe. As a newborn, she is helpless and needs you to protect her. As she grows, she needs your help to explore her environment safely. In the first year, regular medical checkups are important. To keep your baby safe, learn about safety risks for infants. Then take steps to protect your baby from these risks. In this chapter, you will learn about your infant's health and safety needs.

Your Baby's Health

Meeting your baby's health needs is important. You want him to be healthy and strong. You and his health care provider can work together as a team. Your baby needs routine medical checkups. At these visits, the provider will check his growth, health, and development. Your baby will also need special medicines to protect him from certain diseases. Your provider can give him these, too. See Figure 4-1.

Medical Checkups

You may have chosen a health care provider for your baby before she was born. If not, you should choose one right away. This can be a family doctor or a pediatrician. A pediatrician is a doctor whose specialty is caring for babies and children.

You will likely see your baby's health care provider often in this first year. Your baby will have more routine medical checkups in this year than any other. The first examination will occur soon after

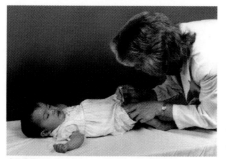

CDC/National Immunization Program

4-1 Getting recommended shots as a baby will protect your child from some serious illnesses.

birth, when you're still in the hospital. The provider wants to be sure your baby is healthy and adjusting well to life outside your body. If any problems are found, they can be treated right away.

The American Academy of Pediatrics suggests infants should also have routine checkups at ages 1, 2, 4, 6, and 12 months. Your provider may want to give your baby more checkups than this. Follow his or her advice—your provider knows your baby's specific health needs.

At routine checkups, the provider will check your baby's growth and development. He or she will also examine your baby from head to toe. This check may include the following:

- ☞ measuring her weight, length, and head circumference to track growth
- ☞ checking soft spots on her head to be sure the skull bones are fusing
- ☞ looking in her ears for fluid or infection
- ☞ testing her hearing and vision
- ☞ looking at her eyes for clearness of the lens
- ☞ tracking her eye movements
- ☞ examining her mouth for signs of tooth development
- ☞ listening to her heart and lungs for heart rhythms, sounds, and breathing problems
- ☞ feeling her abdomen for swelling and tenderness
- ☞ checking her genitals for lumps, tenderness, and development
- ☞ observing her hips and legs for proper movement
- ☞ evaluating her general appearance and alertness

During the checkup, the doctor will ask you a few questions. He or she may want to know about your baby's skills and abilities. When did your baby start to smile, roll over, sit up, or walk? The provider also wants to know about her eating and sleeping patterns. He or she may also ask about the baby's elimination (bowel- and bladder-emptying) habits.

Next, it will be your turn to ask questions. Don't feel shy or embarrassed—asking is the only way you will get answers to your questions. Take a list of your questions with you to the checkup. (You can write these down as you think of them between visits.) The provider may seem rushed, but it's his or her job to answer your questions. If you don't understand the answers, tell the provider so. Also, ask for any information sheets about infant health and development your provider might have.

Immunizations

You'll want to protect your baby from childhood diseases. Most of these pass easily from person to person. Some can be quite serious or even deadly. At your baby's medical checkups, he will get special medicines to protect him from these diseases. These are called immunizations. Most are given in injection (shot) form. Others come in tablet or liquid form.

Each immunization protects your baby from a certain disease. It does this by helping his body make antibodies. These antibodies fight off the germs of the disease. This keeps the disease from hurting the body. After antibodies form, your baby can fight off this disease if he is exposed to it.

For some diseases, one immunization will protect your baby for life. For others, it takes a series of immunizations. These work best when they are given at the right times. See Figure 4-2. This schedule gives an age range when immunizations can be given. Ask your health care provider when to have your baby immunized, and follow his or her advice.

Record the date, dose, and type of each immunization your baby has. It's important to keep an up-to-date record of his immunizations. File this record in a safe place. You will need it to enroll him in a child care center or school.

Immunization Schedule—Birth to 18 Months

Immunization	Age
Hepatitis B	Twice before 4 months 6 to 18 months
Diphtheria, tetanus, and pertussis (DTaP vaccine)	2 months 4 months 6 months 15 to 18 months
Polio (inactivated polio vaccine-IPV)	2 months 4 months 6 to 18 months
Haemophilus influenzae type b (Hib vaccine)	2 months 4 months 6 months 12 to 15 months
Measles, mumps, and rubella (MMR vaccine)	12 to 15 months
Chicken pox (varicella vaccine)	12 to 18 months

American Academy of Pediatrics

 4-2 It's important to keep up with getting your baby immunized. His health care provider can give you an exact schedule for immunizations.

Your Baby's Safety

Many of the accidents that happen in the home could have been prevented. If you understand and reduce safety risks, this will help greatly. First, make sure everyone handles your baby gently. Use caution when holding and providing care for her. Also be careful when you bathe her.

Think about safety when choosing toys, cribs, high chairs, and other baby equipment. Be aware of the possible dangers of these items. Protect your baby from objects in your home that might hurt her. In the last half of the first year, she will be able to move about on her own. As she starts to get into more things, you will have even more safety concerns.

Handling Your Baby with Care

Your baby needs careful handling because he can be hurt very easily. It's fun to play with your infant, but some games are too wild for him. For instance, never throw your baby into the air. This can be dangerous. If you are distracted or look away, your baby could fall. Instead, lift your baby gently over your head. Keep both hands on the baby.

Don't jerk your baby's arms or swing him by the hands. This places too much stress on his elbows and shoulders. It could also cause his shoulder to dislocate. Hold him under the arms and around his chest instead.

<u>Never let anyone shake or hit your baby!</u> No matter what he does, he shouldn't be treated roughly. Your baby can't help crying, messing his diaper, or waking up at night. It can sometimes be frustrating to care for an infant, but you must find other ways to handle these feelings.

Shaking a baby can lead to a serious condition called Shaken Baby Syndrome (SBS). When a baby is shaken, his brain may hit against his skull, causing it to bleed. Over time, this shaking can lead to blindness, brain damage, paralysis, or even death. Even in mild cases, SBS can cause lifelong learning disorders. No one knows exactly how many shakes it takes before a baby develops SBS or what amount of force will cause this condition. For this reason, medical experts strongly advise parents and caregivers never to shake a baby.

Bathing Your Baby

At first, you may be nervous about bathing your baby. You may have many questions. Safety should always be your first concern. Be very careful and always follow the safety points given in Figure 4-3.

In her first week or two, your baby will only need a sponge bath every few days. This is in addition to cleaning her diaper area with every change and wiping her face with a wet cloth at least once a

Bathing Safety Measures

Remember the following safety points when bathing your baby:

❖ Never leave your baby alone for even a second! If you must leave the room, take her with you.

❖ Keep the water shallow (2 to 3 inches at most).

❖ Place a nonskid bath mat on the bottom of the bathtub to prevent slipping. When using an infant tub or the sink, use a towel or blanket to line the bottom.

❖ Use your elbow to check the water temperature before putting your baby in the bath. It should feel warm, but not hot, to you. Your baby needs much cooler bath water than you do.

❖ Turn the water faucet off tightly before putting your baby in the tub. Consider covering the faucet with a towel to prevent burns and scrapes.

❖ Don't let your baby stand in the tub by himself. A fall could hurt him or give him a fear of bathing.

❖ Make sure bath toys are clean, unbreakable, waterproof, and lightweight. Check for sharp edges, tiny parts, or removable parts.

❖ Don't drain the water from the tub with your baby still in the water. The noise and sensation of water going down the drain may scare her.

❖ Be sure to stand in a steady position when you lift your baby out of the bath.

4-3 These safety measures will keep your baby safe during bath time.

day. Your baby's umbilical cord stump is drying out and will soon fall off. Getting the cord wet could slow this process and might allow the area to become infected.

After the umbilical cord falls off, you can bath your baby in a plastic infant bathtub or in the sink. Be sure to line the bottom of the tub or sink with a towel or some padding to keep the baby from slipping. Bathe your baby two to three times a week, or more as needed. Shampooing her hair once a week is fine. Remember to clean her diaper area with every change and wash her face and hands at least once a day. When she begins to eat solid foods, you may need to clean her face and hands after each feeding.

Between three and six months, your baby will grow too big for the baby bathtub. At this time, you can switch to the sink or the regular bathtub. The sink is smaller and not quite as scary for your baby. Until she can sit up well, this might be the easiest. If you switch directly to the bathtub, it might help to put the baby bathtub inside the regular tub for the first few times. This helps your baby get used to the big bathtub.

Once your baby can crawl, she will get much dirtier than before. She'll need a bath every day. Make bath time fun. Let her have some extra time in the bath after washing. Babies enjoy splashing and playing with toys!

Choosing Safe Toys for Your Baby

You will want to provide plenty of toys for your baby to play with. These toys will help him learn and develop. See Figure 4-4. When choosing baby toys, check each one carefully. Safety is the most important point to consider. To check a toy for safety, ask yourself whether the toy:

- ☞ is made of sturdy materials. This means it won't shatter or break easily.
- ☞ is painted with nontoxic paint. Other paints can poison your child.
- ☞ makes any loud noises. These could damage your baby's hearing.
- ☞ has a squeaker that could come off. If so, it's not safe—your baby might swallow it.
- ☞ has any parts that aren't firmly attached. If they're loose, wheels or knobs might be pulled off and swallowed by a child. Check the eyes and noses of any dolls or stuffed animals to make sure they don't come off easily.

 Playing with safe toys under careful supervision is a main way infants learn.

- ☞ has ribbons or cords. These could cause strangling or choking.
- ☞ has any wires, prongs, pins, pointed pieces, or sharp edges. These might injure your baby.
- ☞ has any small parts that could fit into your baby's mouth and throat. You can buy a special tube for measuring small toys. This tube measures 1½ inches in diameter. Toys that fit inside

the tube can also fit in your child's throat. Avoid these toys—
your child might choke on or swallow them. Rattles smaller than
1⅝ inches across can also cause choking. You can also use the
cardboard tube from a roll of toilet paper as a guide.

You should also choose toys that are age-appropriate (designed
for use by someone your child's age). Many toy companies list an age
range on their toy packages or labels. For example, a toy labeled
6 to 18 months would not be age-appropriate for your newborn.
Figure 4-5 lists several toys that are age-appropriate for children in
the first year. Be sure all toys for your infant are labeled safe for
children 3 years and under. To use this label, toys must meet federal
safety guidelines. These toys have no small parts that are likely to
be swallowed or inhaled.

Toy Storage

As a parent, you may wonder how to store your baby's toys
safely. Many parents use toy chests or toy boxes. These items can
pose serious safety hazards. The lid is the biggest danger. A toy
chest lid could close quickly on your infant, catching her hands,
fingers, or head inside. Your baby might also enjoy crawling inside
boxes, tubs, or toy chests. If the lid closed suddenly, she could be
trapped inside her toy chest. Toy tubs or containers without lids are
much safer. You can also store toys in a closet or on a sturdy shelf
or bookcase that cannot be pulled down.

Choosing Safe Baby Equipment

You can buy new baby equipment or borrow it from friends or
family. Used equipment is often sold in want ads, secondhand stores,
and garage sales. The crib is the key item. Playyards, high chairs, gates,
and baby walkers may also be used. The following sections describe
safety features to look for when choosing equipment for your baby.

Cribs

Your baby usually will be unattended when he is in the crib. Be
sure this is a safe place for him. Babies have been injured and even
killed in crib accidents. Falls are the most common injury. In fact,

Age-Appropriate Toys for Your Baby

Birth to Three Months
- Rattles, squeeze toys, teethers designed for this age group
- Plastic or cloth toys designed for this age group
- Bright crib mobile with interesting shapes
- Unbreakable mirror attached to inside of crib
- Books with cardboard, cloth, or vinyl pages
- Bells for baby's wrists or ankles

Four to Seven Months
- Plastic keys or discs on a ring
- Soft balls
- Toys that make quiet, interesting sounds
- Interlocking plastic rings
- Books with cardboard, cloth, or vinyl pages
- Unbreakable mirror attached inside crib or playyard
- Dolls with soft bodies or rag dolls
- Washable stuffed toys
- Crib and activity gyms

Eight to Twelve Months
- Bath toys that float, squirt, or hold water
- Balls of various sizes (but not small enough to fit in the mouth)
- A few large, nontoxic crayons and large paper taped to a surface
- Toys on suction cups
- Simple nesting cups (3-5 cups)
- Stacking ring cones (3-5 rings)
- Simple picture books and rhyme books
- Simple hand puppets (you hold and your baby plays with)
- Simple cars on large wheels (made of flexible plastic with no sharp edges)
- Bell on a handle
- Musical toys, music boxes, cassettes, and CDs for listening

4-5   Choose toys for your baby that are appropriate for his age. These toys are the best ones to help him learn safely.

more babies die in crib accidents than from accidents caused by any other children's product. See Figure 4-6 for a safety checklist to use when choosing a crib.

Choose a safe place for the crib. Do not place it near draperies or blinds. These have dangling cords that could entangle and strangle your child. For this same reason, toys and mobiles that hang across the crib can be dangerous. Remove mobiles from the crib when your

Crib Safety Checklist

Complete this safety checklist about the crib you're considering. If you answer *no* to any of these questions, the crib is not safe. You should choose another crib for your baby.

Yes	No	
		Are the slats on the sides of the crib less than 2⅜ inches apart? (If not, your baby could get part of his body stuck between them.) If you can slide a soda can between the slats, they're too far apart.
		Is the crib's paint lead-free? (If not, your baby risks lead poisoning, which can cause serious disabilities and even death.) Cribs made before 1972 often had lead paint. If you're unsure, choose another crib. If you paint a crib, choose a high-quality, household enamel paint.
		Is the crib free from any sharp edges, splinters, or cracks? (If not, your baby could be hurt. Repair the crib or choose another one.)
		Is there at least 26 inches from the bottom of the mattress to the top of the railing when the mattress is set at its lowest level? (If not, your baby could eventually climb out and fall.)
		Does the mattress fit tightly to the crib on all sides? There should be less than two adult finger-widths of space between the mattress and crib. (If not, your baby could get stuck between the crib and mattress.)
		Are the ends of the crib solid—free from decorative cutouts? (Your baby's head could get caught in a cutout.)
		Do the crib posts stick up less than half an inch above the crib sides? (If not, your baby might get his clothing caught and choke. Don't put your baby to bed wearing a hooded shirt or loose clothing that could get caught on the bed.)
		Are there metal latches holding up the mattress? (If not, your baby could get stuck if the crib has plastic latches that break.)

4-6 You can use this checklist when shopping for a crib. If you answer *no* to any of the questions, this is not a safe crib for your baby.

child is five months old. By this age, he may be able to pull the toy down on himself. He might get tangled in the cord or hurt by the falling toy.

When your baby sleeps, take all pillows, toys, dolls, and stuffed animals out of the crib. This will reduce the risk of him choking and suffocating in his sleep. You can return these to the crib when your baby is awake.

Playyards

You may need to put your baby in a playyard for a few minutes. This can be helpful when you can't watch her as closely as usual. For instance, you might want to cook dinner, take a shower, or work on some homework. Your baby might enjoy moving around in her playyard more than being confined to an infant seat, swing, or crib. You can put toys in the playyard to entertain her.

The playyard does not replace the need for your attention, though. Check on her every few minutes to be sure she is safe while playing in the playyard. Be sure to limit the amount of time your baby stays in the playyard to less than two hours daily. She needs to explore the rest of her environment. Take plenty of time to cuddle and play with her, too.

When choosing a playyard, pick one with tightly woven mesh (with holes smaller than ¼-inch). Inspect the mesh for rips, holes, and loose threads. Check to make sure the mesh is securely attached to the top rail and the floor of the playyard. If there are wooden slats, measure the space between them. Be sure they are placed no more than 2⅜ inches apart. If they're wider apart, your baby could get her hand, arm, leg, or foot caught between them.

Don't put your child in the playyard with one side folded down. This is an invitation for an accident. Your baby might roll out onto the floor or into the space between the mattress and the loose mesh side. She could also suffocate.

High Chairs

You may wonder how to tell if your baby is ready for a high chair. This may depend, in part, on the model of high chair you use. Some of the newer models of high chairs offer reclined positions for infants who cannot sit up on their own. Your baby could use a high chair in the reclined position as soon as he or she is ready to start solid foods such as cereal.

For an older high chair or a model that doesn't recline, your child must be able to sit up on his own. Before this, he might slump to the side or slide down in the seat, which can cause injuries. Waiting until he is ready can reduce the risk of these injuries. Even when he's ready, however, high chairs can be dangerous. They pose a serious risk of falls.

When choosing a high chair, inspect it carefully. See Figure 4-7. Answer the following questions about the high chair's safety:

- ☛ Does it have a wide base so it won't tip?
- ☛ Does it have a three- or five-point harness (restraint similar to that of a car seat) or a seat belt with a crotch strap? A restraint is needed to keep your baby secure in the high chair. No safety straps should be attached to the tray.
- ☛ Does each side of the tray lock into place securely? Check the locks for sharp edges that might scrape you or your baby.
- ☛ Are its safety straps and tray locks easy to use? Check to be sure your baby cannot release safety straps or tray locks from inside the high chair.
- ☛ Is its seat slippery? If so, apply nonskid bathtub decals on the seat to keep the baby from sliding.
- ☛ If it is a folding model, does the high chair have an effective locking device? This will keep it from collapsing while in use.

When your baby is in the high chair, always use the safety straps. Be sure he can't slide down. Babies have slid down in high chair seats and been strangled by the safety straps. Lock the tray in place. Make sure his fingers are out of the way when you lock the tray. Keep the high chair at least 12 inches from a countertop, table, or wall. Your baby could push against these surfaces and tip the high chair over. Never leave your baby unattended in his high chair. Make sure he stays seated at all times. Keep other children from climbing on the high chair.

Gates

Do you have stairs in your home? If so, you may want to use a baby gate. This gate could keep your baby from falling down the stairs. You might use one at the foot of the stairs and another at the top. You might also want to use a baby gate in the doorway of an off-limits room. This would block your baby from going into that room. For example, you may want to keep baby out of the kitchen to protect her from danger. A baby gate can work well there.

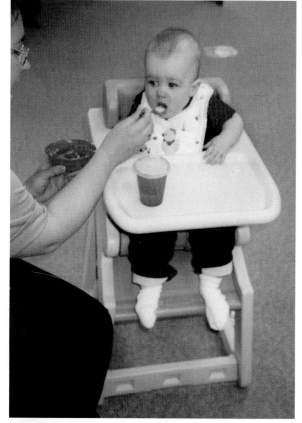

 4-7 Using a sturdy, safe high chair can help prevent accidental falls and injuries.

When choosing a gate, check it carefully for safety. Be sure its openings are too small for your baby's head, arms, or legs to get caught. Make sure the gate doesn't have V-shaped top edges where her head or neck could get caught. Avoid using a gate that is designed to fold or collapse. This type of gate isn't safe. It can easily collapse when your baby leans against or pushes it. Choose a baby gate that will stay secure even when she pushes on it.

Baby Walkers

Are baby walkers safe? This is a question experts are debating. Some think they should be banned because they are unsafe. Other experts think these walkers are safe when used with caution.

Many infants are hurt in baby walkers each year. Your baby can move very quickly in a walker. He can enter a dangerous situation in just a few seconds. The following are common accidents involving baby walkers:

☞ falling down stairs. This can cause serious injury or death.

☞ strangling if baby slides down. His neck can get caught in the straps or the walker itself.

☞ hurting or losing a finger if the walker accidentally folds up.

☞ reaching dangerous objects from the baby's new height. In the walker, the baby might be able to grab cords, cleaning products, cigarettes, matches, or sharp objects the parent hasn't put away.

If you decide to use a baby walker, take several precautions. Watch your baby at all times. Never leave him unattended. Be sure to close the doors to stairways and latch all safety gates. Remove any dangerous objects in your baby's higher reach. Limit his use of a walker to two hours a day. Your baby needs to develop his other muscles, too.

Preventing Accidents

Unintentional injuries are the top cause of death for infants. These deaths are accidental. These injuries fit into several groups. The biggest are motor vehicle accidents and burns. Drowning, falls, and poisonings cause many deaths, too. These deaths might have been prevented with better safety awareness. See Figure 4-8. It suggests ways to protect your baby from these types of injuries. If you are alert and concerned about your baby's safety, you can prevent many accidents. To do this, you must:

☞ think ahead.

☞ know what to expect from your baby (learn about child development).

☞ look at situations from your baby's point of view.

☞ be alert to things that might lead to danger.

Preventing Unintentional Injuries

Burns

❖ Never eat, drink, cook, or carry anything hot while holding your baby.

❖ Don't smoke around your baby or allow anyone to do so.

❖ Always test the bath water temperature before placing your baby in the bathtub. Use your elbow—it's more sensitive than your hands.

❖ Never heat your baby's bottle in a microwave oven. It could heat unevenly and contain "hot spots" that could burn your baby's lips, mouth, and throat.

❖ Don't let your baby crawl near floor heaters, ovens, wood stoves, furnace vents, fireplaces, or barbecues.

❖ Never leave dishes of hot food or liquid near the edge of a table or counter. Your baby can pull teapots, pans, cups, or bowls over onto himself.

❖ Watch for dangling cords to hot appliances, such as a coffeepot, Crock Pot, steam iron, or curling iron. Your baby could pull them down on herself and be burned.

Drowning

❖ Never leave a baby alone in a bathtub. When lying down, an infant can drown in as little as an inch or two of water. If you must leave the room to answer the door or telephone, take your baby with you.

❖ Never leave your baby alone near an open toilet, sink, wading pool, or bucket.

❖ Use caution when taking your baby in a swimming pool, lake, river, or other body of water. Put flotation devices, such as a life jacket and arm floats, on your baby. Keep your hands on him at all times when in the water.

Choking

❖ Check toys often for sharp edges or small parts that could be broken or pulled off.

❖ Keep buttons, beads, coins, and other small objects out of your baby's reach. Pins and other sharp objects are dangerous, too.

❖ Be sure crib gyms, mobiles, or toys strung above the crib are tightly fastened. This keeps the baby from pulling them down and getting tangled. Remove these when your infant reaches five months of age.

❖ Crib toys should not be hung on strings longer than 12 inches. If the string breaks, the baby might strangle himself with the string. Remove drawstrings from hoods and clothing. These can strangle a baby, too.

❖ Never give your baby foods known to cause choking among infants. (Refer again to Chapter 3 for a list of such foods.) Mash or grind all your baby's foods to aid swallowing and prevent choking.

❖ Keep plastic wrap, plastic bags, and dry-cleaner's bags out of your baby's reach. These can cause suffocation.

Falls

❖ Never place a baby in an infant carrier on a chair, table, or counter. If your baby moves, the carrier (with the baby inside) could fall onto the floor. Place the carrier on the floor when you are not right beside it.

❖ Never leave your baby unattended in a high place such as a chair, sofa, table, bed, or crib with the sides down. She could roll off onto the floor.

❖ Use gates at the top and bottom of stairs to prevent your baby from falling down them. Don't allow your baby to crawl on furniture.

Poisoning

❖ Store all medicines and cleaning supplies out of your baby's reach. Use safety latches on drawers and cupboards that contain these and other possible poisons.

❖ Move all plants from your baby's reach. Many types of plants are poisonous.

❖ Be sure all your baby's toys have nontoxic finishes.

4-8 As a parent, it's your job to keep your baby safe from unintentional injuries. To do this, you will need to keep his environment as safe as possible.

You should also be prepared to act quickly in case of an accident or emergency. See Figure 4-9 for a list of phone numbers you may need in an emergency. Keep this list next to each telephone in your home. This way they are handy if you need them quickly.

Childproofing Your Home

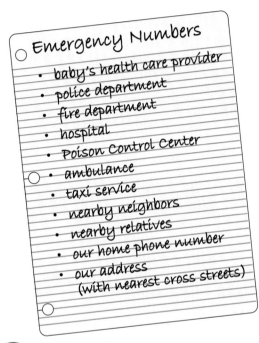

Emergency Numbers
- baby's health care provider
- police department
- fire department
- hospital
- Poison Control Center
- ambulance
- taxi service
- nearby neighbors
- nearby relatives
- our home phone number
- our address
  (with nearest cross streets)

4-9 You can write an emergency contacts list like this one and keep it by each phone in the house.

Your job is to make your baby's world safe. Since most accidents happen at home, it's important to protect her from dangers there. Childproofing means adapting your home to make it safe for your baby. It also means protecting the objects you value from damage by your baby.

Before your baby is mobile, it is easier to keep her from danger. At about age 5 to 6 months, though, she can start to move around. Everything is interesting! Before this time comes, you can start to prepare your home so she can explore it safely. Get down on your hands and knees to look at your home from a baby's point of view. Your home has dangers you may have never noticed! Look for the following:

- ☛ Small or sharp objects. Your baby puts everything in her mouth. To protect her, keep tables and floors clear of anything smaller than 1½ inches. This includes coins, paper clips, staples, nails, cigarettes, pills, tacks, keys, matches, lighters, screws, and other small items. Keep sharp objects like scissors, razor blades, and knives out of her reach, too.

- ☛ Electrical dangers. Cover electrical outlets with plastic plug covers or replace the outlet covers with ones that are child-proof. You can buy these at a hardware store. Keep cords behind furniture and out of the way. Don't let them dangle down over the edges of counters or tables. Your baby could bite them or pull the objects down onto herself. Move fans up high.

☞ Plastic bags and balloons. Your baby can choke on plastic bags and balloons. A bag over her mouth and nose could suffocate her. Never give your baby these items. Tie several knots in plastic bags before throwing them away.

☞ Stairs. Put safety gates on any open stairs. Keep the gates fastened when your baby is nearby.

☞ Small throw rugs and loose carpet. Your baby can trip, slip, or fall on small throw rugs and loose carpet.

☞ Wastebaskets and toilets. Move wastebaskets to closets or cabinets where your baby cannot reach them. This protects her from many unsafe and unsanitary items. Keep your toilet lid and the bathroom door shut. You can also buy a special device to lock your toilet lid so your baby can't open it.

Once your baby can stand, many more hazards are within her reach. Pay attention to what she's doing at all times. Do not leave her alone in a room, even for a minute. Protect your baby by watching for:

☞ Unstable furniture. If your baby tries to pull up on unstable furniture, it might fall on her. Remove furniture that can tip over or fasten it to the wall.

☞ Furniture with sharp edges. Your baby can be hurt falling against the edges or corners of a coffee table. Move furniture with sharp edges out of high-traffic areas. Be aware of furniture with glass tops or doors.

☞ Dangling tablecloths, curtains, or cords (those on electrical appliances or window coverings). Babies can pull these down or get tangled up in them. They can strangle themselves with the cords from window blinds. Be especially careful of blinds or draperies near the crib.

☞ Alcohol. Keep any alcohol in a locked cabinet. It is very toxic to young children.

☞ Medicines, cleaners, pesticides, and other poisons. Keep these products locked away from your baby. Use childproof latches on cupboards in the kitchen, bathroom, and laundry.

☞ Stoves, ovens, portable heaters, hot plates, and candles. Teach your baby to stay away from hot things and open flames. Take steps to keep these items out of her reach. Turn pot handles toward the back of the stove so your baby can't pull them down onto herself. Hot liquids can scald her.

- ☞ Doors, windows, and screens. Use locks and safety latches to keep these closed.
- ☞ Water heaters. Adjust the hot water temperature in your home to 120°F. This helps protect your baby from burns.
- ☞ Recliners. Always keep the chair in its upright position when it's not in use. Don't let your baby play on the leg rest, even when an adult is sitting in the chair. Her neck, head, arm, or leg could get trapped between the leg rest and chair if the chair folds up.
- ☞ Firearms. Guns kept in the home are dangerous. Many children die each year in gun-related accidents. If you can, rid your home of all guns. If not, keep the guns unloaded and locked away. Lock the bullets away in another place.
- ☞ Valuables and precious things. Move these objects to higher areas or pack them away until your baby is older. This makes it easier for both of you.

Car Seats and Car Safety

Among infants and young children, car accidents are the most common cause of unintentional injury. In fact, these accidents are the leading cause of death in this age group. For this reason, car seats are required by law in all 50 states. However, many parents do not use these seats properly. The most common mistakes they make are: threading the seat belt through the car seat or seat base incorrectly; failing to use the restraints or not using them correctly; and not using the car seat on short trips.

Most fatal car accidents occur within five miles of home. These cars are usually not going more than 25 miles an hour when the crash occurs. A car seat is the only way to protect your baby from this risk. You must use it correctly <u>every time</u> your baby rides in a car. In a crash, the car seat can keep him from being thrown into the windshield or dashboard. It also protects him from being hurled against other people or pitched out the window. A car seat also keeps your baby secure so the driver can focus on driving.

There are three important aspects of car seat safety. These are: choosing a safe car seat, installing the seat properly, and using the seat correctly. Each is vital to protecting your baby.

Choosing a Car Seat

Choosing the right car seat for your baby can be confusing. You want a seat that is safe, affordable, and easy to use. Most importantly, choose a federally approved car seat. <u>Never</u> use any type of seat that doesn't meet these requirements. Don't use an infant carrier as a car seat, even if it has harness straps. An infant carrier is not built to protect an infant in a car crash. (Here, the term <u>infant carrier</u> means a piece of equipment designed for use only in carrying a child. It is safe to use only for this purpose.)

You will also want to choose a seat that has not been recalled (found to be unsafe) by the manufacturer. To check on recalls, you will need to know

- ☞ the seat's manufacturer
- ☞ manufacture date
- ☞ model number
- ☞ serial number

You should be able to find this information on the box that contains the seat or in the display information at the store. It can also be found on the label located on the seat. The label also usually gives a toll-free number for the manufacturer. Call the manufacturer to inquire whether the seat has been recalled. You can also check for recalls by calling the Department of Transportation's Auto Safety Hotline.

If possible, avoid used car seats altogether. Even a minor accident can damage a car seat and make it ineffective. This type of damage may not even be visible. However, if you choose a used car seat, make sure of the following about the seat:

- ☞ there are no broken or missing parts
- ☞ it was never in an accident
- ☞ it is no more than six years old (older seats may not meet today's safety guidelines)

☛ it has not been recalled

☛ the owner's manual is available (call the manufacturer if you need another copy)

Choose a car seat that is right for your baby's weight and size. The two options for babies are infant car seats and convertible car seats. An infant car seat is used only until your baby weighs 20 to 22 pounds or is 26 inches long. It is convenient because it has a handle for carrying. Some infant car seats also have a base that stays secure in the car while the seat can be unhooked for carrying the baby. An infant car seat must only be used in the rear-facing position. A convertible car seat is used in the rear-facing position for newborns and babies and in the forward-facing position for heavier infants and toddlers. It stays in the car rather than being removed as a carrier.

Pick a car seat that is easy for you to use. It should fit easily into your car. See Figure 4-10. Look for a harness that is easy to fasten and unfasten. It should also be easy to adjust the harness while the seat is installed.

A main difference among car seats is the type of harness. Infant car seats have two types of harnesses: the five-point and the three-point. The five-point harness is the most effective. It has five straps—two at the shoulders, two at the hips, and one at the crotch. It also has a plastic harness clip that holds the shoulder straps at the chest and two metal tongues that slide into the buckle on the crotch strap. The three-point harness has two shoulder straps that connect in a V-shape at a metal tongue that snaps into the buckle on the crotch strap.

Convertible car seats offer the five-point harness, a T-shield harness (two shoulder straps attached to a padded T-shaped or

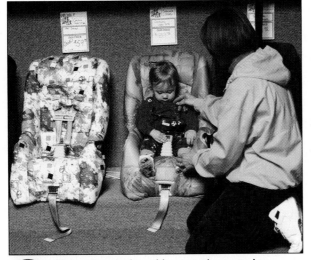

4-10 Take your baby with you when you're shopping for a car seat. Try getting her in and out of the seat. This will keep you from buying a hard-to-use seat.

triangular shield that fits into the buckle), or an overhead shield harness (a padded traylike shield that swings down over the child's head and snaps into the buckle). For a young infant, a five-point harness offers the most protection. T-shields and overhead shields are too big to protect smaller babies well.

Installing a Car Seat

After choosing the right seat, next you must install it correctly. When putting the car seat in, follow the manufacturer's instructions exactly. If you misplace the car seat owner's manual, call the manufacturer for a replacement. This should be sent to you at no cost.

Read your vehicle owner's manual for instructions about using a car seat in your car. There may be important instructions specific to your car. Follow these instructions exactly. Contact the vehicle manufacturer if you need another copy of this owner's manual. It can be sent to you, but there is usually a charge.

From reading your vehicle owner's manual, find out which is the safest spot in your car for the car seat. This is almost always in the center of the back seat. (For some cars, another location may be safer.) Infants and young children should never ride in the front seat. This is especially true if the car has a passenger-side air bag. In a crash, a child in the front seat (even in a car seat) can be hurt or killed by the inflating air bag.

Next, check out your car's seat belts. Note what type of seat belts your car has, because this may affect the installation. For instance, some seat belts require a locking clip, a metal device that holds the seat belt (and car seat) securely. Your vehicle owner's manual or dealer can tell you whether a locking clip is needed. Many new car seats come with locking clips. Certain cars, however, need a special heavy-duty locking clip. If you need one of these, you can get it from a dealer at little or no charge.

Install your infant's car seat in a rear-facing position. Federal law states babies who weigh less than 20 pounds or are less than 26 inches long must face the rear. This is the safest position for them. You may be able to keep the car seat in a rear-facing position even longer than required by law. This will depend on the maximum rear-facing weight listed on the car seat. Keeping the seat in a rear-facing position until this weight is safer than turning it to face the front too soon.

When the car seat is in the right position, put your knee in the middle of the seat or seat base and press down with your body weight. This will hold the seat or seat base firmly against the seat of the car. Thread the car's seat belt through the correct holes in the car seat or base. Be sure the seat belt stays tight. Use a locking clip, if needed. Once fastened, you should not be able to move the seat or seat base more than one inch in any direction. (If it moves more, reinstall the car seat properly.) If the seat has a top tether strap, be sure it is secured correctly. (If not, the seat will fly forward in a crash.)

If you use a convertible car seat in the rear-facing position, eventually you will need to turn the seat to face the front. Before you do this, though, reread the owner's manuals for the car seat and the vehicle. Learn how to properly install the seat in this position. Be sure both the car seat and vehicle seat belt are secured correctly.

Using a Car Seat Correctly

Once it is installed, you must use the car seat correctly. See your car seat owner's manual for usage instructions. Fasten the restraint as directed. The straps should be snug and flat against the baby's body. They should not be twisted. Only one of your fingers should fit between your baby's body and the harness. Keep the plastic harness clip level with your baby's armpits. This helps hold the baby's head and body against the seat in a crash.

You may need to adjust the car seat's restraints to your baby's size. Read the directions to learn how to tighten or loosen the harness. Also, be sure the shoulder harness comes through the right slots. For an infant seat, use the slots that are level with or just above the baby's shoulders. For a convertible seat, use the slots that are level with or just below your baby's shoulders. To move the harness up or down a slot, consult the car seat owner's manual. See Figure 4-11 for other important tips about car seat use.

Using a Car Seat Correctly

Keep the following points in mind when using your baby's car seat:

❖ You may need to pad the sides of the car seat with rolled towels or a support pad to protect your young baby's neck and head. This support is very helpful while your baby is too young to hold his head straight.

❖ Never start the car until your baby is strapped into the car seat. Ask everyone in the car to wear a seat belt. Otherwise, in an accident, they could be flung about and hit your baby.

❖ Keep heavy objects and tools in the trunk of the car. In a crash, objects inside the car can fly about and hit your baby.

❖ Never leave your baby or young child in the car alone for even a minute. Your baby might feel abandoned or lonely. He may also get overheated or too cold quickly. Babies left in a car on a hot day have died in less than an hour. A baby might also be kidnapped while waiting in a car for the parent to return.

❖ Never leave your baby in the car with other young children unsupervised. Another child might play with the car controls, start the car moving, and cause an accident. This child might accidentally lock all the children in the car.

❖ When driving, stop the car if you need to attend to your baby. Pull to the shoulder of the road or a parking lot. Reaching into the back seat of a moving car to meet your baby's needs could affect your ability to drive safely.

4-11 Following these tips will help you use your car seat more safely.

All these tips, rules, and guidelines may seem like a lot to remember. They are important, though. With time and practice, you will feel confident in meeting your baby's health and safety needs.

Major Points

☛ To protect your baby's health, take her to see her health care provider regularly. She needs several routine medical checkups in her first year. At these visits, her provider will check her health, growth, and development.

☛ Your baby needs to be immunized. This prevents him from getting dangerous childhood diseases. He needs to get these immunizations on a certain schedule, based on his health care provider's advice.

☛ Handle your baby with care. Don't play games that are too rough for your baby. Don't shake him or hit him, either. If you do these things, it could permanently injure or even kill him.

☛ When bathing your baby, never leave her unattended. Take other precautions at bathtime to protect her safety.

☛ Choose your baby's toys carefully. You will want to select toys that are safe for your baby, as well as age-appropriate.

☛ The improper or unsafe use of common baby equipment has harmed or killed infants. Take precautions when choosing and using this equipment. Be aware of safety features and regulations regarding baby equipment.

☛ Preventing accidents is an important aspect of safety. Many babies die needlessly each year in accidents. The most common are motor vehicle accidents, burns, drowning, falls, and poisoning.

☛ You're responsible for making your baby's world safe. Childproofing means making needed changes in your home to protect your child from danger.

☛ Car accidents are the leading cause of death for infants and young children. Car seats are required in all 50 states. The safest place for a baby is in the middle of the back seat in a car seat facing backward.

Chapter 5 Your Toddler's Physical Development and Needs

Your baby is growing. Once he can walk well on his own, he is said to be a toddler. The toddler period usually lasts from ages one to three years. It's an in-between stage. Your toddler is moving rapidly away from being a baby. He is becoming a child.

During the toddler years, your child becomes more independent. He wants to do things for himself, and can start learning how. You can teach him to brush his teeth and hair. Let him learn, but help when needed. In these years, children also start learning to use the toilet.

Your toddler's food, sleep, and clothing needs are also changing. He wants to feed and dress himself. See Figure 5-1. You can begin to teach him how. Caring for your active toddler is both challenging and rewarding!

Your Toddler's Physical Development

Your toddler will continue to grow at a rapid rate. However, she won't grow as quickly as she did before. No one grows faster than a baby! Your toddler's proportions are changing pretty quickly. By the time she's three, your toddler will look more like a child than a baby. (To learn more about your child's physical development, see the Developmental Milestones chart at the end of this chapter.)

Height

Your toddler's height will keep increasing at a fairly steady rate. At one year, your toddler is about 30 inches tall. As a two-year-old, he will be about 34 inches tall. By his third birthday, he will

grow to about 38 inches tall. After age three, your child will grow 2 to 3 inches a year until adolescence. See Figure 5-2 to learn more about average heights in the toddler years.

Here's an interesting fact—you can predict how tall your toddler will be as an adult. Your daughter will reach about half of her adult height at 18 months old. Your son will reach about half of his adult height at 24 months old.

Weight

During the toddler years, the average amount of weight gain slowly decreases. Your child keeps gaining weight, but not as quickly as before. Refer again to Figure 5-2.

5-1 In the toddler years, children begin learning to feed themselves and handle other tasks on their own.

Between ages one and two, your child will gain five to six pounds. From two to three, she will likely gain four to five pounds. Your child will keep growing at a steady rate of about five pounds each year in childhood.

Average Height and Weight of Toddlers

Age	Height		Weight	
	Boys	**Girls**	**Boys**	**Girls**
12 months	30 in.	29¼ in.	22¼ lb.	21 lb.
18 months	32½ in.	32 in.	24½ lb.	24 lb.
24 months	34½ in.	34 in.	27¾ lb.	26¼ lb.
30 months	36½ in.	36 in.	29¾ lb.	28¾ lb.
36 months	38 in.	37½ in.	32 lb.	31 lb.

5-2 Your child gains height and weight more slowly in the toddler years than during infancy. Keep in mind the figures given are only averages.

Body Proportions

Your toddler's looks will change more than his size. His body proportions are changing. Your child will keep developing from head to toe and from the trunk outward. His trunk, arms, and legs grow longer. Your toddler is constantly in motion, so his baby fat starts to disappear. His arms, legs, and face are slimmer.

Finally, your child's body grows at a faster rate than his head does. This gives him a less top-heavy look. At birth, your baby's head was one-fourth of his height. At two years, it is only one-fifth of his height. By age three, your toddler looks more like an older child. See Figure 5-3.

 Your three-year-old is starting to resemble an older child. His body proportions are becoming more adultlike.

Teeth

At 12 months, your baby has about six teeth. The first set of molars usually comes in between 12 and 15 months of age. The second set comes in between 20 and 24 months. By 30 months, most toddlers have a complete set of 20 teeth.

When the molars are coming in, it can make your child uncomfortable. She may be very fussy. Sucking often makes the gums hurt even more. Offer drinks from a cup instead of a bottle. Give your child something cold and hard to bite on.

You might think your toddler's baby teeth don't matter. After all, she will lose these teeth eventually. These teeth are important, though. Suppose she loses them early due to decay or infection. The permanent teeth won't be ready to replace them. Other baby teeth will shift to fill the gap, leaving no room for the permanent teeth.

The health of your toddler's teeth depends partly on her diet. Eating nutritious foods in her first two years helps her build strong teeth. Calcium-rich foods such as whole milk, cheese, cottage cheese, and yogurt are very helpful in building strong teeth.

Avoid giving your child foods that promote tooth decay. These include candy, soda, and sugar-coated cereal. Sweet foods can stick to her teeth and cause decay. Never put your child to bed with a bottle of milk, juice, or sweetened fruit drink. The acids and bacteria in these drinks can pool in the mouth and cause a serious form of tooth decay. This decay can affect both her baby teeth and permanent teeth.

Brain Development

In the toddler years, your child's brain continues to grow rapidly. By age four, his brain will be three-fourths of its adult size. As your child's brain becomes more developed, he can pay attention for longer periods of time. This allows him to learn many new tasks.

At about two years of age, the brain begins to specialize. Each area of the brain controls specific parts and functions of the body. At this time, your child begins to prefer using one hand over the other.

As the parent of a toddler, you can influence your child's brain development. Offer your toddler plenty of chances to practice his new skills. Praise and encourage him. Allow him to explore, and make sure his surroundings are safe. Protect him from negative influences that might interfere with his brain growth.

Large and Small Motor Skills

Your child's large and small muscles are still developing. Your child is still refining her large and small motor skills. See Figure 5-4. Large motor skills allow her to walk, run, sit, stand, and jump. Small motor skills include picking up a small toy, scribbling, or turning the pages of a book.

A milestone in small motor development for toddlers is handedness. This is a preference for using one hand more than the other. As early as 18 months, your child may start using either her right or left hand most of the time. This isn't a decision she makes—it is set by the brain. Don't try to change her hand preference. That could cause learning problems. Once you know which hand your child prefers, encourage her to use this hand. For instance, when you give her a toy or spoon, put it in her preferred hand.

Delays in Physical Development

Each child develops at his own rate—some more slowly than others. This is normal. Your child will likely learn new physical skills at about the same time as his peers. By learning the average age ranges for an activity, you'll know when a skill is likely to develop. If your child

Hermanda Gleason

 This toddler's increasing large motor skills allow her to ride this tricycle.

develops much more slowly than the average, call his health care provider. The following are also signs your child might have a delay:

- ☛ Your toddler isn't walking by age 18 months.
- ☛ He can't walk and push a wheeled toy at the same time by age 2.
- ☛ After walking for many months, he walks only on his tiptoes or doesn't walk heel-to-toe.

Your local health department or school district might offer a yearly child development screening. If so, you could take your child to it at little or no cost. At this screening, his hearing, vision, and speech will be tested. He will also be screened in each area of development. This will reveal any delays. Your health care provider should know whether this type of screening is offered in your area.

Providing Physical Care for Your Toddler

Toddlers are very active, and they want to be independent. For this reason, their physical care needs change. You can use this time to start teaching your child self-care skills. These are the skills she will need to take care of her own physical needs. These include washing her hands, caring for her hair, bathing, dressing, eating, and toileting.

As your toddler becomes busy with exploring, it may be more of a challenge to keep her clean! The earlier you start teaching the importance of hygiene (personal cleanliness), the better. The best way to teach self-care skills is by example. Be sure you practice good hygiene yourself.

Hand Washing

Washing your hands is an important habit. It rids your hands of germs that can make you sick. It also helps you keep clean. Teach your toddler to wash his hands before eating. He also needs to wash them after the following:

- eating
- touching the nose or mouth; blowing or wiping the nose
- handling a pet
- playing outside
- using the toilet

Be consistent. Don't forget to have your child wash his hands at these times. This will help him form the habit more quickly.

When he's first learning, he will need plenty of help. Soap up your hands, too. Wash each other's hands. Make a game of it. Who has the cleanest hands? Be sure your toddler always uses soap and spends enough time washing. (Sing the song "Happy Birthday" twice. This is the length of time experts suggest you should spend washing your hands.)

Once he knows how, you can encourage your toddler to wash his own hands. You should still supervise, though. Put a small stepstool in the bathroom so he can reach the sink easily. Be sure he knows which is the hot water and which is the cold. Adjust the water temperature of your hot water heater to 120°F so the hot water won't burn your child.

Tooth Care

Now is the time to start teaching your child to brush her own teeth. She can learn to hold the toothbrush and move it across her teeth in a gentle motion. Your toddler still hasn't reached the right stage developmentally to clean her teeth by herself. Some experts say the small motor skills she needs for brushing won't be fully developed until age 7 or 8. Until then, she will still need your help with this task.

Help brush her teeth twice a day. Always brush before bedtime so food particles don't stay in the mouth overnight and cause tooth decay. See Figure 5-5 for suggestions to develop a good tooth care routine for your toddler.

Tooth Care Tips for Toddlers

❖ Let your child watch you brush your teeth. This will help him understand what you are doing when you brush his teeth.

❖ Give her a child-sized toothbrush with small, soft bristles. Allow her to use the toothbrush first, and then finish brushing for her. If she won't let you hold her brush, get two brushes—one for you to use with her and one for her to hold.

❖ Use only a pea-sized amount of toothpaste. If your toddler doesn't like the taste of toothpaste, try a new brand or just use water for a while. At this age, brushing and rinsing are more important than using toothpaste.

❖ Clean each tooth thoroughly, top and bottom, inside and out. Direction of brushing really doesn't matter at this age.

❖ Floss your child's teeth once a day. You can start this when she has her full set of teeth.

5-5 Beginning a tooth-care routine now will help your child develop lifelong dental hygiene habits.

Young children tend to focus on the teeth they can see—their front teeth. Make a game out of "finding and brushing the hidden teeth." Be sure to give her a new toothbrush every three months.

Your toddler will need to make her first trip to the dentist. Some experts suggest a first dental visit between one and two years of age. Others say it's okay to wait until between two and three years of age.

To prepare your child for her first dental visit, talk to your child about what to expect. Tell her you will stay with her during the visit. You may also want to take her to a routine dental visit with you. Then she can see the dentist's office and what the dentist does. It may make her excited for her own visit. Reading a children's storybook about the dentist may help, too.

After the first visit, your toddler should have a dental checkup once every six months. These routine checkups and cleanings can prevent future dental problems. They can also start your child on a lifelong path to good dental health and hygiene.

Bathing

As a toddler, your child may be eager to start washing himself. You can show him how. If possible, give your child his own special sponge or washcloth. Teach your child to use soap and wash all body parts carefully.

Even if your toddler can wash himself, baths should still be carefully supervised. Don't leave your child alone in the bathtub for any reason. He could slip or fall. He could be injured or drown. Your child might get soap in his eyes or try to turn on the hot water. Cover the faucet handles with a towel to protect him from burns and scrapes. Watch your child at all times in the bath. Most children are not old enough to bathe alone until they reach school-age. Even then, you should remain nearby, listen carefully, and check on your child from time to time.

Make bathtime fun for your toddler by making it playtime. You can make a game out of washing. Name the body parts with your child and make up bathtime songs. Special bath toys can also add to the enjoyment. See Figure 5-6. Some toddlers like bubbles in the bath. For others, bubbles can irritate the skin.

Bonnie Mori

5-6 This toddler enjoys playing in the bath as long as she has all her favorite tub toys. Notice the cover over the faucet.

Hair Care

Your toddler's hair gets dirty during everyday activities such as playing and eating. At the same time, your active toddler may not like having her hair washed. The following tips should make hair washing more enjoyable:

- Use a tear-free baby shampoo. This kind of shampoo won't burn your child's eyes. Still, you should try to keep the water and soap from getting into her eyes.
- Give her choices when you can. Does she want to lean forward or backward for washing? Does she want to hold a sprayer to wet her own hair? Does she want to wash her hair in a shower or bath?
- Make hair washing fun by creating funny hair styles with the shampoo.

Many parents keep their children's hair short. This makes it easier to keep the hair clean, combed, and brushed. Tangles can make combing uncomfortable for your child. If you keep your child's hair longer, you might buy a hair care product made for detangling the hair.

Give your toddler her own comb and brush. She may enjoy combing and brushing her hair. It can help her feel more independent and grown up.

Nail Care

Keep your child's fingernails and toenails cut short. Shorter nails are easier to keep clean. They also help your child avoid scratching himself or others. His nails will grow quickly, so trim them once a week. Nail-cutting tips include the following:

- ☛ Cut nails after a bath. Wet nails are softer and easier to cut.
- ☛ Use nail clippers or blunt-ended scissors for safety.
- ☛ Place your child on your lap to keep him from wiggling.
- ☛ Cut toenails straight across.
- ☛ Follow the natural line of the fingernails. Do not cut too close to the skin.

Toilet Learning

Between 30 to 36 months is a good time for most children to begin toilet learning, which is often called potty training. At this age, muscles in the bowel and bladder areas are developed enough so your child can control them. Before your child can control these muscles, she isn't ready. If you try to teach her before she's ready, both you and your child will likely be frustrated. Most children learn to control their bowels first, and then their bladders. By age five, most children can tend to their own toileting needs independently.

Signs your child is ready for toilet learning include the following:

- ☛ Bowel movements occur on a fairly regular schedule.
- ☛ Her diaper stays dry for two hours or more. This means her bladder can store some urine.
- ☛ Your child wants to use the toilet.
- ☛ She can follow directions and is eager to please you.
- ☛ Your child shows interest in imitating other family members in toileting.
- ☛ Your child knows when her bladder is full or a bowel movement is about to occur. She tells you with words, facial expressions, or behaviors.
- ☛ She can walk to the bathroom and remove her clothing quickly.

When your child is ready to start toilet learning, place a potty chair in the bathroom or in her room. Let your child sit on the chair for a few weeks with her clothes on. Explain what a potty chair is used for and when to use it.

Once your child wants to sit on the potty chair, remove the diaper. Show her how to plant her feet on the floor. This is important for a bowel movement. Make the potty chair part of your child's routine once or twice a day for a week for so. Remove her full, dirty diaper and let the bowel movement fall into the potty chair. This helps her understand what the potty chair is for.

Let your child play near the potty chair without a diaper on. Remind her to use the potty chair when needed. When she succeeds in using the potty chair, reward her with praise.

Daytime control of bowel movements usually comes before bladder control. When your child's bladder matures, you will notice her diaper is not wet after a nap. At this time, you can start asking your child to empty her bladder before naptime. Once your child can do this, you can begin to teach your child to empty her bladder on the potty chair. To do this, your child must

- ☞ want to use the potty to urinate
- ☞ know ahead of time so she can wait while her clothes are being removed

Your child cannot hold a full bladder very long. Remind her to go to the bathroom at regular intervals, such as every hour.

Many accidents will happen. Just clean your child and change the wet clothing. Take a spare set of clothing when you and your toddler leave the house. Scolding your child will not help when accidents occur. This just makes her feel unhappy, clumsy, and inadequate.

Once your child uses the potty regularly, you can switch to training pants during the day. Your child will welcome this sign of growing up. It may make her feel special.

Bed wetting is very common for children younger than age five. Be patient—all children have accidents. Your child can't help this—it is beyond her physical control. Do not blame your child for these accidents.

Meeting Your Toddler's Food Needs

A toddler's food needs are different from those of an infant. Your child isn't growing as quickly as before. He will also use some of the fat he stored in infancy. As a result, your toddler may be less hungry, and he will eat less overall.

Your toddler's appetite will vary from day to day. Some days he will be hungry all day long. On other days, he won't eat much. This is normal! Your goal as a parent is to promote healthy eating. Your feeding responsibilities include the following:

- buying, preparing, and serving your child a variety of healthful foods.
- setting mealtimes and snack times.
- setting a good example by eating a variety of foods.

Your toddler has responsibilities, too. His jobs include the following:

- choosing which foods to eat from those offered.
- deciding how much of the offered foods to eat.

If you keep these responsibilities in mind, you can avoid battles with your toddler. Toddlers often say no and want to be independent. Don't get into a power struggle with him about eating. He can decide how much and what to eat. Sometimes he may choose not to eat at all. This may disappoint you, especially if you spent a lot of time preparing the food. Calmly accept your child's decision not to eat. Do not feed him anything else until the next scheduled mealtime or snack time. Your child will not suffer from missing one meal or snack.

Food Guide Pyramid for Young Children

You may be familiar with the Food Guide Pyramid, a simple-to-use guide for healthful eating. A second version, called the Food Guide Pyramid for Young Children, shows the daily food needs of children ages two to six years old. See Figure 5-7. You can use this Pyramid when planning meals and snacks for your toddler. She needs to eat foods from each main food group every day. In the sections that follow, you will learn about each of these food groups.

USDA Center for Nutrition Policy and Promotion

5-7 You can use the Food Guide Pyramid for Young Children when planning meals for your toddler. Offer two- and three-year-olds less in each serving than indicated, except for milk.

Grain Group

The grain group includes breads, crackers, cereals, rice, and pasta. All these products come from grains. Grains are a major source of energy. Whole-grain products offer the most nutrition. Your toddler needs more servings of grains than any other food group. He needs six servings from this group daily.

Vegetable Group

Vegetables are a good source of vitamins and minerals. You may purchase fresh, canned, or frozen vegetables and serve them cooked or raw. Foods such as broccoli, tomatoes, potatoes, carrots, corn, peas, green beans, cabbage, and lettuce are in this group. Peppers, bok choy, onions, mushrooms, okra, and spinach are also vegetables. Your toddler needs three servings from the vegetable group daily.

Fruit Group

Fruits are also rich in vitamins and minerals. Offer your child a variety of fresh, canned, cooked, or dried fruits. Examples are apples, bananas, berries, melons, oranges, peaches, pears, pineapple, and strawberries. You can also give your toddler a serving of fruit juice each day. Don't give her much more fruit juice than that—large amounts can cause diarrhea. Your toddler needs two servings from the fruit group daily.

Milk Group

This group contains milk and other dairy products, such as cheese, yogurt, pudding, ice cream, and cottage cheese. Your toddler can start drinking cow's milk after his first birthday. See Figure 5-8. Until he is two years old, offer whole milk (not fat free or reduced fat milk). Young toddlers need the fat that whole milk

Tera Nakai

5-8 Toddlers can drink milk from a sippy cup. They need two servings of milk a day.

provides. After your toddler turns two, switch to reduced fat milk, lowfat milk, or fat free milk. This will reduce his total fat intake. Your toddler needs two servings from the milk group each day.

Meat Group

The meat group includes beef, pork, chicken, turkey, fish, beans, eggs, nuts, and peanut butter. Offer your child a variety of foods from this group. Lean meats and beans are good choices. Avoid nuts and spoonfuls of peanut butter. These are choking hazards for toddlers. Your toddler needs two servings from the meat group daily.

Fats and Sweets Group

Fats and sweets are in the small triangle at the tip of the Pyramid. Chips, candy bars, cookies, snack cakes, and soft drinks are some examples of fats and sweets. Also included are gravy, cream sauces, oils, dressings, and mayonnaise. Limit the amounts of these foods your child eats. Offer these foods only occasionally and in small amounts. They do not offer anything healthful to the diet.

Serving Sizes

Toddlers need smaller servings than adults. A good rule of thumb is one tablespoon per year of age. For instance, a two-year-old would need two tablespoons and a three-year-old would need three tablespoons. Give your child less than you think she will eat and let her ask for more.

See Figure 5-9 for a one-day sample menu for a two-year-old. This menu meets the requirements of the Food Guide Pyramid for Young Children and offers the correct serving sizes.

Snacks

Your toddler has a small stomach. He needs to eat more often than three meals a day. The following is a good eating pattern for a toddler:

- ☛ breakfast
- ☛ midmorning snack

☞ lunch
☞ midafternoon snack
☞ dinner
☞ bedtime snack (if needed)

Snacks help provide the extra energy and nutrients your child needs. Choose healthful snacks, such as fruits, vegetables, yogurt, or whole-grain crackers. Avoid giving fats and sweets for snack time. These are not healthful choices.

Sample Menu for a Two-Year-Old

Food	# of Servings	Group
Breakfast		
½ ounce of ready-to-eat cereal (low-sugar)	1	Grain
½ cup of milk (2% or less fat)	½	Milk
¾ cup of orange juice	1	Fruit
Morning Snack		
3 to 4 whole-wheat crackers	1	Grain
½ cup of milk	½	Milk
Lunch		
½ turkey sandwich on whole-wheat bread	1	Meat
	1	Grain
¼ cup pretzels	1	Grain
½ apple (sliced)	1	Fruit
½ cup of milk	½	Milk
Midafternoon Snack		
2 tablespoons (⅛ cup) of carrot sticks	1	Vegetable
½ cup milk	½	Milk
Dinner		
½ cup of cooked pasta	2	Grain
1 to 2 ounces of baked chicken	1	Meat
2 tablespoons (⅛ cup) of peas	1	Vegetable
2 tablespoons (⅛ cup) of corn	1	Vegetable
Water		

5-9 This sample menu for a two-year-old meets all the requirements of the Food Guide Pyramid for Young Children. You can plan menus like this to be sure you are providing your toddler enough of the foods she needs.

Avoid giving a snack just before mealtime. This will dull your child's appetite. Instead, offer the snack at least one hour before mealtime. Mealtime is also more pleasant if everyone eats together and your child is hungry.

Self-Feeding

Most toddlers are eager to feed themselves. The first few months are a messy time. Spills occur. Spoons and cups are sometimes turned over. This is how your toddler learns to feed himself. You may feel frustrated by his messiness and strange eating habits. Don't let your negative feelings show. You don't want your toddler to stop trying. See Figure 5-10 for common eating behaviors in the toddler years.

As he grows, your toddler will become a little neater and have better manners. Until then, it's up to you to make mealtime as pleasant as possible. The tips on the next page may help.

Common Eating Behaviors of Toddlers

15 Months	18 Months	24 Months	36 Months
has a limited ability to self-feed	has a decreased appetite	has clear food choices	has an increasing appetite
mostly uses fingers to feed self	refuses foods, food choices waver	prefers foods separated, not mixed	eats a greater variety of foods; food choices are not so strong
uses spoon, may dump food out on the way to the mouth	has an improved ability to self-feed	can self-feed more easily	self-feeds very well
will accept help with feeding if it is offered	accepts help less often	refuses help unless tired	rarely wants feeding help

 Does your toddler show any of these common eating behaviors? Try to be patient—in time, he will outgrow them.

☞ Keep mealtimes on a regular schedule. Your child finds it difficult to wait for food when hungry.

☞ Place the high chair near the table. Put newspaper or plastic under the high chair for spills. Use a booster chair when your child is big enough to sit at the table.

☞ Use a plastic bib with a pocket at the bottom to catch spills.

☞ Give small amounts of food. Your child will ask for more if he is still hungry.

☞ Fill cups or glasses only one-fourth full. This way there is less to spill.

☞ Use child-sized, unbreakable spoons and forks.

☞ At each meal, serve some finger foods and some foods requiring a spoon or fork. This allows your child to practice without becoming too frustrated.

☞ Keep mealtime pleasant. Praise your child. Try not to criticize him. His manners will improve.

☞ Be a good role model in manners and food choices.

Eating Problems

Sometimes meals don't go smoothly. Your toddler may test you, and you may have some food-related battles. For example, he may refuse to try new foods. He may be a picky eater and only want to eat one or two favorite foods. Your patience and understanding will go a long way at this time. Your child is asserting his independence.

Introduce new foods early. The older your child gets, the more likely he is to refuse a new food. Offer a new food when your child is hungry. Don't give up if he doesn't try it the first or second time. The more he is exposed to a food, the more likely he will try it. You may have to offer it at 5 to 10 meals before he will taste it. He is more likely to taste a new food if he sees you eating it. Nagging him makes him less likely to eat. Your toddler may also be more interested in new foods when he is not overly tired.

Your child will test you by refusing to eat some foods. The best thing you can do is try not to overreact. Your toddler may want to eat only one or two favorite foods. This is called a food jag, and it is normal. Be careful not to promote this behavior. If your toddler wants a certain food every day, give it to him at snack time.

Don't ask your toddler what he wants to eat. Instead, prepare his plate and put it on the table in front of him. Provide a variety of healthful foods for each meal. Serve only a very small portion of new or disliked foods. One spoonful of peas can look less intimidating than a heap of them. Offering this small portion size will also minimize waste.

Choking is still a problem for toddlers. Your toddler is still learning to chew. At times, he may gulp his food without chewing it carefully. The risk of choking is quite high. It's also important to avoid foods that are likely to cause him to choke. Refer again to Chapter 2 for a list of these foods.

Choosing Clothing for Your Toddler

Your toddler is active. He needs clothing that will protect him. It must be comfortable, safe, and durable, too. You must also consider the cost. Include the cost of shoes in your clothing budget. Since your toddler walks, runs, climbs, and jumps, he will need to start wearing shoes.

Your toddler may also be ready to start dressing and undressing himself. This is a big achievement. It makes him proud of himself. You can encourage him to practice this new skill.

Protection

You want your toddler's clothes to protect her skin and keep her warm, dry, and safe. Long pants protect your child when she crawls or falls. Choose garments with reinforced knees and elbows. These garments will protect your child, and they will last longer. On dresses and overalls, active children need shoulder straps that are wide enough to stay on the shoulders. You should also choose fabrics that stretch. If your child's clothing is too stiff or tight, it may rip easily.

Comfort

As with infant clothes, you want your toddler's clothes to be comfortable. Soft fabrics feel nice against the skin. Clothing that is a little loose is comfortable. Tight or stiff clothing may keep your child from moving freely. If it is too big, it may be unsafe and uncomfortable. Your child will let you know which clothes he finds uncomfortable. These are the ones that cause him to fuss and squirm. He may even tug at an uncomfortable garment or pull it off himself!

Durability

Choose clothing that is durable, or sturdy and long-lasting. Very active children need sturdy woven or knit fabrics. Thinner fabric may tear easily. Check a garment's knees, pockets, and seams to see if they are reinforced. This helps the clothes last longer. Stitches that are too long or uneven will unravel. Clothes with these problems will not last as long.

Self-Dressing Features

Choose clothing your child can put on by herself. Look for clothes that fasten in the front rather than on the side or in the back. Elastic waistbands are easier for your child to handle than belts. As your child starts to use the potty chair, elastic-waisted, stretchy pants, and two-piece outfits are ideal. See Figure 5-11. Neck openings need to be large enough for easy dressing. Large buttons, zippers, and snaps are simpler for your toddler's small fingers.

 The zippered neck on this shirt and these elastic-waisted pants make dressing easier for this toddler.

Safety

Safety is also important when choosing your child's clothing. Sleepwear is required by law to be flame-retardant. This means it can't catch fire easily or burn quickly. Long drawstrings, skirts, scarves, and sashes are dangerous. They can get caught in doors, wheels, and play equipment. This can cause choking or serious injury. Be sure buttons, fasteners, and trim are attached securely. Otherwise, these can be pulled off and swallowed. Bright, colorful clothing helps drivers and parents see a small child more quickly.

Care

Choose clothes for your toddler that offer easy care. Children's clothing should be easy to wash and dry. It shouldn't need ironing. Check the care labels to learn what type of care a garment requires.

Cost

Children's clothing can be expensive. Toddlers are still growing quite rapidly. Check for deep hems and cuffs. These allow you to move the hems out, enlarging the clothes. Look for clothing on sale or at discount stores. Shopping at garage sales, thrift sales, used clothing stores, and secondhand stores is a good way to save money. Many families and friends exchange children's clothing to cut clothing costs.

Shoes

Your child's shoes should fit properly to prevent damage to the foot. Check your child's shoes regularly. Your child can't tell you if the shoe is too short or narrow. Too-small shoes can cause permanent damage to the feet even if your child isn't fussing or complaining. Young children's feet can be squashed without causing pain.

Shoe size is measured by having the toddler stand with the weight on that foot. Both length and width must be measured. For a proper fit, half an inch of space should remain between the ends of the toes and end of the shoe. This gives your child's feet a little room to grow. Younger toddlers often change shoe sizes every three months. Between two to three years, children change shoe sizes about every four months.

Learning Your Toddler's Sleep Patterns

As your toddler becomes older, naptimes may change, and less sleep is needed. Your toddler may also resist going to bed at night. Toddlers don't want to miss out on anything! Getting your child to take a nap or go to bed may become a challenge. See Figure 5-12.

5-12 Once your toddler is finally asleep, he looks precious! He hardly seems like the same person who was refusing to take a nap just a few minutes earlier.

Naps

As your toddler gets older, she may not want to sleep at naptime. Even if she doesn't sleep, she needs to rest. Have your child lie down or sit still. She could read a book or play a quiet game. Sometime during the toddler years, your child will probably give up her morning nap. Then she'll be down to just one nap in the afternoon.

Bedtime

Your toddler probably won't like to go to bed. He may ask for one more glass of water, kiss, or bedtime story. As he gets older, he will use more verbal requests and tricks to avoid or delay going to bed.

Notice when your child shows signs of being sleepy. Make this his regular bedtime. Use a bedtime routine to quiet and relax your child. Include a bath, reading a story, and quietly talking. Make this a peaceful, calming, and soothing time. Let him sleep with his security objects (favorite soft toy or blanket). Your toddler should be awake for your good-night kiss when you leave the room.

Some children feel separation anxiety at bedtime. Your child may cry when you leave the room. Allow him to cry for 10 minutes or so. If he's still crying, go back to him. Try settling him down again and then leave for 10 minutes more. You may have to do this a number of times and a number of nights. Be consistent and stay calm. Don't scold your child. Do not reward his behavior by feeding him or staying with him.

For some children, this battle at bedtime is a way to get your attention. Your child may climb out of bed and come to you. Be firm but loving. Tell him it is time for bed now and take him back to bed. Your toddler will soon learn he has nothing to gain by getting up. Then he will start staying in his bed and going to sleep.

Nighttime Awakening

In these early years of life, you can never be sure your child will sleep through the night. Some toddlers sleep all night for a few days or even weeks and then begin waking every night. Nighttime awakenings are often caused by a change in a routine. See Figure 5-13.

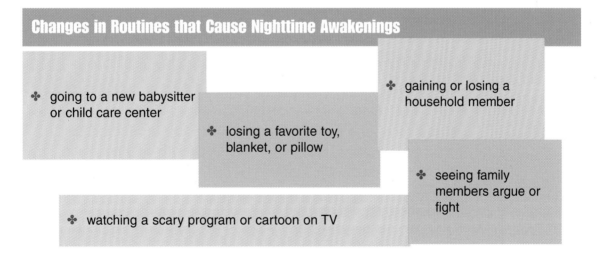

Changes in Routines that Cause Nighttime Awakenings

❖ going to a new babysitter or child care center

❖ losing a favorite toy, blanket, or pillow

❖ gaining or losing a household member

❖ seeing family members argue or fight

❖ watching a scary program or cartoon on TV

5-13 If your toddler starts waking during the night, think about changes in your routine that may be causing him trouble sleeping.

Between 12 and 14 months of age, your toddler will start to actively dream. This can startle your child awake and frighten her. Bad dreams and nightmares are common among toddlers. As your child gets older, she has a more active imagination. Older toddlers may think a shadow looks like a bear, a monster is in the closet, or a snake is on the floor.

If a nightmare or bad dream wakes your toddler, comfort and hold her. Ask about the dream. Stay with your child until she is calm enough to fall asleep.

Your child will have more nightmares when she is under stress or feels anxious, troubled, or fearful. Try to keep the tension level down in your home. Talk to your child to help keep her troubling feelings from building. This helps your child cope with stress, shows you care, and comforts her.

Moving from Crib to Bed

When your baby is 35 inches tall, he is too big for a crib. He can now easily climb out of the crib, which could cause a dangerous fall. It is time to move your baby to a toddler bed.

Many children are excited about sleeping in a big bed. It makes them feel more grown up. If your child is a little nervous about sleeping in a bed, start by using the bed for naps. After your child feels more comfortable, place him in the bed for the night.

☛ Toddlers grow more slowly than infants. As they add height and weight, their body proportions change. By age three, your toddler will look more like a child than a baby. As her brain develops more, she can pay attention for longer periods of time. Your toddler will spend many hours building both her large and small motor skills.

☛ You can begin to teach your toddler about good hygiene. He can learn to meet his hand washing, hair care, tooth care, and bathing needs. Self-care skills are important.

☞ Toilet learning should begin when your child shows signs that she's ready. Most children start at about 2½ years old. Your child will learn to control her bowels first. Bladder control is easier in the day, but eventually occurs at night, too. Many accidents will occur.

☞ Your toddler will take fewer naps, but still needs some rest during the day. A bedtime routine will help him go to sleep. Your toddler will start to actively dream. These dreams may awaken him. Your toddler should move from a crib to a bed when he's about 35 inches tall.

☞ Use the Food Guide Pyramid for Young Children to help you select foods for your toddler. Choose the right number of foods from each group daily. Your toddler will need smaller serving sizes because her stomach is small. She will also need snacks between meals.

☞ Your toddler will feed himself most of the time. To express his independence, he may refuse to eat or want only a certain food. Patience and understanding will help at this time. Try not to get into power struggles with your child over food.

☞ When choosing clothing for your toddler, consider protection, comfort, durability, self-dressing features, care, and cost. Your toddler will also need to start wearing shoes.

From 12 to 18 Months, I

* stand and walk alone. I walk with stiff legs and shift my weight from side to side as I walk. To keep my balance, I place my feet wide apart and toddle.
* run without falling as often.
* like to explore and follow you from room to room. I don't stay in one place for long—I'm always on the go.
* may throw or roll ball. I may walk into a large ball when I'm trying to kick it.
* can jump with both feet.
* pull or push a toy while walking.
* stoop to pick up a toy without losing balance.
* walk up and down stairs with help.
* climb onto furniture.
* build a tower of 3-4 blocks and then knock it down.
* turn book pages several at a time.
* like to fill and empty containers.
* can hold two or three objects in one hand.
* pick up tiny objects with my thumb and index finger. use my index finger to point.
* try to fit objects inside one another.
* scribble with a crayon.
* feed myself and hold my cup to drink.
* have definite food likes and dislikes.
* fuss when it's time to go to bed at night.
* take a shorter morning nap than I used to.

From 18 to 24 Months, I

* am improving my coordination and my large and small motor skills.
* can walk backwards and sideways.
* throw a ball overhand instead of tossing it.
* may kick a ball without falling or tripping over it.
* show the first signs of dancing as I move my body in response to music.
* can take a few steps on my tiptoes.
* sit in a small chair by myself.
* enjoy playing on the swings and other playground equipment with your help.
* can drop objects of various shapes into the correct holes in a shape sorter.
* take toys apart and put them back together.
* can open doors, unwrap packages, and help with simple chores.
* enjoy finger painting and scribbling with big crayons. I also like to play with clay.
* build a tower of six or more blocks.
* start to prefer one hand over the other.
* may hand you my cup when I'm thirsty.
* take off my shoes and socks; unzip zippers.
* may brush my own teeth, but I still need your help. You can brush them after I do to be sure they're clean.
* can wash and dry my hands with help.
* may be able to put on my clothes if they have easy-to-use fastenings.
* might put my dirty clothes in the hamper or my toys away if you ask me to.

(Continued)

From 24 to 30 Months, I

❖ can play on swings, ladders, and playground equipment with less help. I still need you to supervise closely, though.

❖ can kick a ball forward. This is possible because I can now stand on one foot for short periods of time.

❖ climb up and down from furniture without help.

❖ jump from a low step.

❖ climb stairs. I often bring both feet to the same step before going to the next step. I hold onto the wall, railing, or your hand for support.

❖ throw objects overhand.

❖ run fairly well.

❖ may enjoy dancing to music.

❖ can carefully turn book pages one at a time.

❖ pour and play with water.

❖ button large buttons.

❖ carry toys from place to place.

❖ can tear paper into tiny pieces. You can give me old newspapers or magazines to practice this skill.

❖ can imitate many of the marking you make on paper, such as lines, circles, and crosses.

❖ may unscrew lids and turn knobs on doors and stereo.

❖ may or may not be ready to start toilet learning. I might start to ask to go to the toilet, but I'll still have lots of accidents.

❖ should be served whatever the family is eating. I can choose which foods on my plate to eat and how much I want to eat.

❖ may dress myself with a little help.

❖ may switch from a crib to a bed. Please be consistent but patient—this can be a hard adjustment for me.

❖ can soap and rinse my own hands and arms easily.

From 30 to 36 Months, I

❖ improve my walking and balance even further.

❖ climb on the jungle gym.

❖ walk up and down stairs with alternating feet.

❖ run, jump, and hop easily; enjoy running games.

❖ pedal tricycle with good steering.

❖ can catch a large ball with my arms and hands out straight.

❖ bend over without falling down.

❖ throw and fetch all kinds of objects.

❖ kick and throw balls of all sizes.

❖ can string smaller (½-inch) beads. Supervise closely when I'm doing this—you don't want me to put these small beads in my mouth.

❖ put together simple puzzles with 6 to 12 pieces.

❖ learn how to hold a pencil as if to write.

❖ love to draw with chalk or crayons.

❖ paint with enthusiasm using a paintbrush or my hands.

❖ begin to cut with child safety scissors with your supervision.

❖ am improving at self-help skills like brushing my teeth, eating, and washing myself as you watch and assist.

❖ put on and remove most of my clothing.

❖ use a spoon and fork well, but I often forget to chew my food completely.

❖ can probably go to the potty by myself as long as the light is on.

Chapter 6
Your Toddler's Intellectual, Social, and Emotional Development

To understand your toddler's actions and emotions, consider how she thinks and feels. A young toddler has a short memory. She can't think very far ahead. For example, she might climb up on the counter, but forget how to climb back down.

Because your toddler can't think ahead, she can't wait. She wants everything right now—this instant. Your toddler may tell you she wants a cookie. She may start crying because she can't wait long enough for you to open the package.

Your toddler is well aware she's a separate person from you. After about 18 months of age, she can recognize her image in a mirror. She wants to be independent. Even the words she uses show she has developed a sense of self. Her favorite words may include <u>no</u> and <u>mine</u>.

Your Toddler's Intellectual Development

Your toddler gains intellectual skills at a fast rate. Both heredity and environment help develop these skills. Heredity decides what your child's potential will be. Environment affects whether he can reach that potential. You are a key part of your child's environment. It's up to you to promote his intellectual growth. Giving your child your attention is vital. He learns when you listen, talk, and play with him each day. Toys and books will also shape his development.

Attention Span

Your child's attention span slowly increases in the toddler years. Attention span is the length of time your child can focus on one object or activity. For instance, your one-year-old is interested in everything she hears, sees, smells, tastes, and touches. She can't focus on one thing for long. She is distracted easily. As a three-year-old, your child will pay attention longer. She has learned to concentrate and tune out distractions. She will be able to listen to a longer story or play longer with a toy. See Figure 6-1.

This longer attention span promotes learning. To remember and learn a skill, your child must first give it her full attention. She must focus on the task in order to practice it. Be sure you have your child's attention before trying to teach her something. If she becomes distracted, you might stop and wait for her attention again. After a minute or so, if she hasn't returned her attention to the task, it's probably best to let it go for now. You can try again another time.

 As a toddler, your child can concentrate longer on an activity such as coloring. Her attention span is longer.

Memory

Memory is a key part of your child's intellectual development. It allows him to learn. By repeating an action or an event, your child starts to remember it. This memory is stored and can be retrieved at a later time. When the action or event happens again, his memory will help him know what to expect.

Your child's memory starts working when he's a baby. As he grows, his memory gets longer and longer. When your child is a one-year-old, he will remember daily routines for feeding, changing, and going to bed.

By age two, your child has an even better memory. He will look several places for a favorite toy even if he didn't see where you put it. Your child will tell others what you did when you went out together. He might say you went to the grocery store or park. Your child will remember a babysitter or family member he hasn't seen in a few weeks. By age three, your child can remember simple directions and a few colors. He can recall more past events. Your child's memory will continue to increase throughout childhood.

Forming Concepts

In the toddler years, your child will keep herself busy forming concepts. A concept is a general idea formed from other information and details. Your child must remember quite a few details to form a general concept.

As your child compares objects, she forms concepts. Between 18 and 24 months, she will start to sort objects. Your toddler may look at, feel, or hold objects as she studies them. She may group together the objects that are alike, and set any unlike objects aside. Suppose your toddler groups all the large toys together. This shows she is starting to understand the concept of size.

Most toddlers form the following basic concepts:

- size (big or little)
- direction (up and down, over and under)
- shape (square, triangle, or circle)
- sound (phone, cat, or car)
- smell (orange, banana, toast, or toothpaste)
- texture (smooth, rough, soft, hard)
- temperature (hot, warm, or cold)
- volume (how much sand or water a cup or pail can hold)
- time (breakfast, lunch, naptime, bath time, bedtime, day, and night).

You can encourage your child as she starts to form these concepts. See Figure 6-2 for some ways to help your toddler learn about shape, sizes, sounds, and volume.

Helping Your Toddler Form Concepts

Shapes

❖ Match shapes on different household items.

❖ Make or buy a shape-sorter toy.

❖ Offer various shapes of finger food (cheese cubes, sandwich squares, and banana slices).

Size

❖ Compare your shoe and your child's shoe. You can also compare your hands, height, and clothes.

❖ Play with sets of pots and pans, measuring spoons, and mixing bowls that fit inside one another.

❖ Put toys into groups by whether they are big or small.

Sounds

❖ Bang on an empty oatmeal box with a wooden spoon and with your hands.

❖ Fill and empty salt box with beans or rice. Tape the box shut for safety. Shake the box.

❖ Clap pot and pan lids together.

Volume

❖ Play dump and fill games in the bathtub using water and various tub toys.

❖ Pour liquid into and out of different sizes of cups.

❖ Pack sand into different sizes of pails in the sandbox.

6-2 You can offer simple activities that will reinforce the concepts your toddler is learning.

Intellectual Aspects of Play

A toddler's play helps develop his mind. Through play, your child learns to think, explore, and form new concepts. He gains so much from play that some experts call play children's work. Play is one of the main ways your child learns about his world.

Play promotes brain growth. It also helps your child refine his small and large motor skills. It can stimulate his imagination. Using crayons, blocks, sand, or clay allows him to be creative. Other toys, such as puzzles and games, build your child's thinking skills. Figure 6-3 lists some age-appropriate toys for your toddler.

You can help your child learn by playing with him. Follow his lead rather than taking over. For example, when you play cars together, let him make all the "rules." Let him decide which car each of you will use. Ask him where the cars are going. If he makes sounds for the cars, you can do the same. This will let your child know what he thinks is important to you. It will also help him enjoy play more.

Developing Language Skills

Children's language skills develop at a fast pace in the toddler years. Between ages one and three years, your quiet baby will turn into a chatterbox full of questions. She will be able to tell you what she wants much more of the time. You won't have to guess as often.

Learning to talk is part of your toddler's intellectual development. She needs to learn words so she can think and

Age-Appropriate Toys for Toddlers

* balls of various shapes and sizes
* bath toys (boats, containers)
* blocks
* board books, storybooks and magazines
* cars, trucks, planes, and trains
* outdoor toys (sandbox, swings) and digging toys (pail, shovel)
* dolls of various sizes
* push and pull toys (doll carriages, shopping carts, wagons)
* toys that encourage pretend play (kitchen sets, play lawn mower, dress-up clothes, toy telephone)
* nesting toys
* rhythm instruments (bells, cymbals, drums)
* music tapes and CDs for listening, singing, and dancing
* puzzles (4-5 pieces to 6-12 pieces)
* simple shape sorters
* stuffed animals and puppets
* unbreakable mirrors

6-2   As your child grows, he needs different types of toys to help him learn.

communicate clearly. Your child was born without knowing even one word. She made many sounds before saying her first word. Now she's a toddler who can say quite a few words.

Talk to your toddler often. She learns to talk by listening to you. Your child will model the words you say. After age one, you can stop using baby talk with her. This kind of talk could harm her language development. Speak clearly. Use short sentences. Name and describe objects for her, such as <u>yellow banana</u> or <u>blue shirt</u>. Use pointing and facial expressions to make yourself clear. Allow her to respond. If your child starts a conversation, stop and listen. Suppose you're often impatient or don't make eye contact when she talks to you. Your child may get discouraged and give up trying to talk to you.

Vocabulary grows rapidly in the toddler years. See Figure 6-4 for the average numbers of words toddlers use. Most toddlers have a growth spurt in their vocabularies at 19 to 24 months. Your toddler may learn as many as 10 to 20 new words each week. By age two, she may know as many as 200 words. Toward the end of her toddler years, your child will also improve her use of language. For instance, she will start to use pronouns (I, me, you), plural words, and verb tenses (jump, jumped, will jump) correctly.

In general, girls learn language a little faster than boys do. Many girls start to talk earlier, and they string sentences together sooner than many boys. Each child develops at his or her own rate, though. Don't worry if your child doesn't match the average. Many children are a little ahead of or behind these numbers. You should be

A Toddler's Expanding Vocabulary

Age	Average Number of Words Used
12 months	3
18 months	22
24 months	272
36 months	896

6-4 It may seem like your toddler is having a vocabulary explosion. Keep in mind the figures given are only averages.

concerned only if your child is far behind the average. Talk with you're child's health care provider or a speech professional if you have concerns.

Reading Books

Reading stories to your child is a great way to build language and listening skills. Children love to have books read to them. It teaches them new words and concepts. Reading time can also be a quiet, special time between parents and child.

Tera Nakai, GRADS student at Newcomb High School

6-5 Mom can spark her toddler's curiosity about books by reading a new story to him.

Choose a book and story that fits your child's age. One-year-olds like short, simple books with big, colorful pictures. Two-year-olds like stories about familiar things, such as a puppy or going to the park. Three-year-olds like stories that are a little longer and have a plot.

Most likely, your child will have a few favorites. He will want you to read these stories again and again. You may feel bored by this repetition, but your child does not. He can learn something new each time. Read familiar stories often, but include new ones, too. See Figure 6-5. Vary the pitch of your voice while reading. Use facial expressions and body movements to act out the story.

When reading to your child, let him do the following:

- ☞ sit on your lap or close beside you
- ☞ look at the pictures as long as he wants
- ☞ point out the words and pictures that go together (the word <u>cow</u> and a picture of a cow)
- ☞ ask questions about the pictures or story
- ☞ turn the pages

Creating and Telling Stories

Another good way to boost your child's language skills is to create and tell stories with her. Your stories can be as long or short as you like. They can feature pets, people your child knows, or a favorite toy. When creating a story, use the following tips:

- ☛ Start the story with "Once upon a time..." to get your child in the mood.
- ☛ Include some action right at the start and keep the story moving.
- ☛ Have a goal, like saving the cat from danger.
- ☛ Give your story a happy ending.

You may want to let your older toddler help make up the story. This can build her verbal and creative skills. If she seems to get stuck, offer ideas or ask questions to keep the story going. Both you and your child will enjoy this time together.

Your Toddler's Social and Emotional Development

Much social and emotional development occur in the toddler years. Your child is becoming an individual. He has a mind of his own and no longer depends upon you completely. Your toddler has a wide range of emotions and learns how to express them.

Your toddler is becoming independent, too. He has a need to develop a sense of autonomy. Autonomy means being able to rely on yourself. It is a feeling that he can do some things without any help. As a result of this autonomy, your toddler will feel pride and develop self-control. If he doesn't develop it, he will start to feel doubt and shame. This will affect his social and emotional development throughout life.

Your toddler's independent spirit drives much of his behavior. You will often hear him say some version of the words, "I can do it myself." This extends to walking, talking, eating, dressing and toileting. Your child feels proud when he does these things on his own!

Your toddler looks to you to show him how to behave in a new situation. He observes your facial expressions, body language, and tone of voice. If you smile and encourage him, he will approach the new situation. If you seem upset, he will stop what he's doing, cry, or return to you. Your child looks to you for support and security in a strange situation.

Between ages two and three, self-control begins to appear. Self-control means being able to resist the impulse to use inappropriate behavior. Give your toddler simple rules. Make these relate to safety, not damaging things, and not harming people. Give her simple chores.

Self-Awareness

Your toddler is learning more about herself as a person. Your toddler wants to be independent. She's aware of herself and her needs. She shows you this when she does the following:

- ☛ talks about her feelings. She learns to talk about her own feelings using words such as <u>love</u>, <u>hurt</u>, <u>cry</u>, and <u>bad</u>. You can promote this by asking how she feels and helping her find words to express these feelings.
- ☛ recognizes her own facial features. She can identify herself in a mirror or picture. You can build this by showing her pictures of herself and others. Point out the features that make her special.
- ☛ shows she knows her own abilities. Your child knows what tasks she can and can't complete alone. You can help by asking whether she needs help before taking over a task for her. If the activity is safe, let her try. Remind her to ask for help when she needs it.
- ☛ follows rules of conduct. Your child is beginning to understand there are things she should do and should not do. Make your rules clear and be consistent. Explain why a rule is needed and what might occur if it's not followed. Praise your child for following the rules. Remind her when she forgets.

If your child does what she should, she will call herself a <u>good girl</u>. A <u>bad girl</u>, she reasons, does something naughty. Help her separate her behavior from her view of herself. Writing on the wall with a marker is bad behavior, but it doesn't mean your child is a bad person. If your child calls herself bad girl, tell her, "No, you're not a bad girl, but it's wrong to write on the walls. We write on paper. Would you like some?" Let you child know you love her even when she misbehaves.

Awareness of the Feelings of Others

In the toddler years, your child starts to notice that other people have feelings, too. See Figure 6-6. He may say others are happy, mad, sad, bad, scared, good, or loving. Your toddler starts to understand that his actions can affect the feelings of others. For instance, he may say you are happy because he kissed you. He starts to learn it makes you upset when he misbehaves.

6-6 Your toddler is learning about other people's feelings. This makes him a more sensitive playmate.

Your child may also react to how others feel. He may show empathy, or an understanding response to the feelings of others. Suppose your toddler sees his friend Joey crying. In response, he may give Joey his favorite teddy bear or pat his face. Your child wants to help his friend feel better.

Your toddler notices how you feel, too. He may pat, hug, or comfort you if you seem sad or quieter than usual. By doing this, your toddler shows he cares how you feel. Praise your child when he shows empathy. This is a sign of a caring person.

Temper Tantrums

At one time or another, most toddlers have temper tantrums. Temper tantrums are outbursts of negative emotions and behavior. During a temper tantrum, your child may cry, scream, kick, hit, or hold her breath. She may lay on the floor and refuse to get up. At this time, your toddler is overcome by her strong feelings. She can't control her behavior. Your child is not aware of anything else that is going on around her.

Temper tantrums are common between ages 18 months and 4 years. They are the result of your toddler's built-up anger, stress, and frustration. When your toddler is angry and frustrated, she is full of tension. Her feelings must be released. Since she can't put these feelings into words, they come out in her actions.

Toddlers often have tantrums when they can't do or have something they want. To prevent some of these tantrums, remove tempting objects you don't want your child to have whenever you can. Try to keep your child away from situations you know will frustrate him.

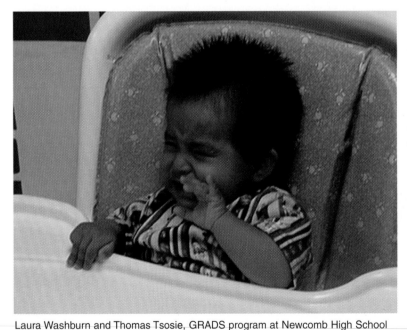

Some tantrums happen when a child is very tired or hungry. See Figure 6-7. If your child falls asleep after the tantrum, chances are she was tired. Keep your child on a regular schedule for eating and sleeping. Avoid taking her someplace when she is tired or hungry. These actions will reduce the chances of this kind of tantrum.

Less often, your child's tantrums may be a way for her to get

Laura Washburn and Thomas Tsosie, GRADS program at Newcomb High School

6-7   Toddlers find it hard to wait for food, which can sometimes set off a tantrum.

your attention. In this case, give your child the attention she wants right away. This may cut the tantrum short. Change your position to be eye-level with your child. Look her in the eyes and tell her you're listening. Ask her what is wrong, and what she needs. Tell her you love her. Make an effort to give your child more attention so she doesn't ask for it by throwing a tantrum.

If you suspect your child often uses tantrums as performances, you might try ignoring the tantrums. Stay nearby, but don't get involved except for safety reasons. Look away, or go into the next room if you can. When your child sees you aren't focusing on the tantrum, she may move onto something else. If the tantrum occurs for another reason, ignoring it may make it worse. This may make your child feel you don't care or her feelings don't matter.

During a temper tantrum, safety is important. Keep your child from being hurt or hurting others. Use a time-out or put her in her bed. You may need to pick your child up and hold her in your arms until she calms down. This can protect both her and other children. The comfort of your arms may help your child unwind from the tantrum faster, too.

When she's having a tantrum, your child needs you to remain calm. She needs your help to regain control. Be understanding. Talk softly and comfort her. Avoid having a temper tantrum yourself. Don't hit, spank, or yell at your child. These actions don't show respect for your child's feelings. Secondly, they may make a tantrum last longer. Finally, remember your child learns behaviors from watching you. You will want to teach him more positive ways of dealing with problems.

Don't respond to the tantrum by giving in to your child's demands. Suppose the tantrum started because your child wanted a cookie. You told her no for a reason, so don't back down. Giving her the cookie now teaches her that tantrums work. Your child will repeat this behavior in the future to get her way.

After your child is calm again, talk about the tantrum. Explain that kicking, biting, and throwing things are not proper behaviors. Tell your child you didn't like what she did, but that you will always love her. See Figure 6-8 for more helpful tips on dealing with temper tantrums.

Handling Temper Tantrums

To prevent a tantrum from occurring:	After a tantrum starts:
Consider what your child wants and needs.	Stay calm.
Talk softly to your child. Use a friendly tone of voice when you ask your child to do something. Remember to say <u>please</u> and <u>thank you</u>.	Keep your child from getting hurt or hurting anyone else. Remove any objects that might cause physical harm.
Don't punish your child for saying <u>no</u>. Just repeat your request calmly and clearly.	Don't argue. During a tantrum, your child can't think or reason. Talk in a calm, soothing voice. Don't scream back-this could make the tantrum last longer.
Offer choices whenever possible. Let him pick which toys to play with, which pajamas to wear, or which story to read.	Don't reward your child by giving into his demands. This will teach her that a tantrum is a good way to gain your attention and have his own way.
Avoid situations that trigger a tantrum. Suppose she always has a tantrum at the store. If possible, leave her with a family member the next time you go shopping.	Remove your child from the situation. If the tantrum happens in public, calmly carry him to the restroom or car.

6-8   It's best to prevent a tantrum before it starts. If one occurs, your response can make a difference in how long it lasts. You can use these tips to prevent and handle temper tantrums.

Toddlers' Fears

Fear is a normal, healthy emotion felt by people of all ages. Your child has fears, too. A person's fears change over time. You don't have the same fears as your toddler, so you may think his fears are silly. Actually, his fears are just as real as yours—he just fears different things. For instance, his fear of the dark bothers him just as much as you might fear snakes or spiders.

After two years of age, your toddler will start to have more fears. He's more intellectually advanced and aware of more things to fear. Common fears of toddlers include injury, wild animals, startling noises, storms, monsters, and bad people.

Fear has a good purpose. It helps protect your child. Fear keeps him from getting into many dangers. When he is fearful, he will quickly seek you for security and support. This way you can protect him, too.

You can learn much about your toddler's fears by watching and listening closely. Pay close attention to your child's cues. When your child is afraid, he may become very quiet. He might also cry or scream quite loudly. This depends on his temperament. Your toddler might also act out his fears in his play. For instance, he may growl like a wild dog or pretend to be a monster. Your toddler might pretend he is protecting a favorite stuffed animal from the feared object.

To overcome his fears, your child needs your emotional support. Be patient, calm, and understanding. Talking to your child about his fears may help. For instance, you can explain that thunderstorms bring the rain that helps the grass and flowers grow. Figure 6-9 offers some tips for dealing with your child's fears.

Conquering Your Toddler's Fears

Do	Don't
prepare your child for new experiences. If your child fears dogs, let him know before going to a house with a dog. Tell your child how he should act. Give him a pleasant experience with a calm and friendly dog who is good with children.	laugh at your child or scold her about her fears.
encourage your child to talk about her fears. This may help her resolve them.	treat your child as if his fears aren't serious.
offer simple, honest explanations for events and situations that frighten your child.	talk to others about your child's fears when she can hear you.
role-play with your child the situation he fears. Help him think of possible solutions for facing his fears.	let your child watch TV just before bedtime. This can cause bad dreams.
help your child learn what is real and what is imaginary. This will happen gradually over time.	force your child into the situation he fears. Encourage him but don't push.

6-9 Your child's fears are very real to him. Be sensitive to his feelings when dealing with his fears.

Social and Emotional Aspects of Play

Play promotes your child's intellectual growth. It also builds social and emotional skills. Play is an important part of your child's life. It's also very fun!

Watch your toddler as she plays. You will see she uses play to express her feelings. She may do this using puppets or dolls. Through pretend play, your toddler may act out her feelings. Suppose your child feels sad. She may hold her doll close and say the doll is sad. Art activities are also good for expression. They allow children a creative outlet for their feelings. For instance, your child might express feelings she cannot describe in words in her painting.

Play allows your toddler to interact with others. See Figure 6-10. She starts to learn about sharing and taking turns. It gives her a chance to practice her language and social skills. Through play, your child can learn to negotiate and solve problems. She can start to make friends. With pretend play, your toddler can experiment with what it's like to be someone else. This is an important part of empathy. Your child also uses play to form ideas about family, career, and gender roles. In one day, your child might be a mother, father, daughter, son, friend, firefighter, president, office worker, teacher, or nurse. These are just some of the social aspects of your toddler's play.

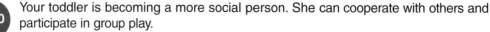
6-10 Your toddler is becoming a more social person. She can cooperate with others and participate in group play.

Major Points

☛ Your toddler continues to develop intellectually at a fast rate. His attention span increases and his memory improves. These skills aid him in forming basic concepts such as size, shape, texture, volume, and direction.

☛ Play promotes intellectual development. It teaches your toddler about objects, people, and the world through play. Through play, she also learns how to solve simple problems.

☛ Developing language skills is a big part of your toddler's intellectual development. He will learn many new words and start to talk in short sentences. He understands more words than he can say. To boost his language skills, read him books and tell him original stories.

☛ Social and emotional development are rapid in the toddler years. Your toddler needs to build a sense of autonomy. She will feel many new feelings. You can teach her good ways to express them. She will learn to play better with others and develop some self-control.

☛ Your toddler shows he is more aware of himself and others. He talks about his feelings, recognizes himself, knows his own abilities, and learns about right and wrong. He may start to show empathy by comforting others who are upset.

☛ Temper tantrums usually begin shortly before age two. These occur mainly because of built-up anger and frustration. Safety is important during a tantrum. Be calm, patient, and understanding. When your child can express herself better, these tantrums should pass.

☛ Your toddler may become afraid of more things during the toddler years. This is because he is more aware of his surroundings, some of which may scare him. Assure your toddler you will protect him from what he fears. Remember his fears are very real to him.

☛ Play has social and emotional aspects, too. Through play, your toddler learns to express her emotions. She can pretend to be someone else, which allows her to explore the roles of others. Your toddler learns to play with others and share.

From 12 and 18 months, I

❖ learn by exploring objects.

❖ like to feel different textures with my fingers.

❖ start to form concepts.

❖ will usually come to you if you call my name.

❖ respond to simple directions.

❖ am more interested than before in scribbling with crayons.

❖ will repeat actions many times to see if I get the same results.

❖ use simple problem solving to reach a goal.

❖ learn by watching you that every object has a purpose. I enjoy using toys that have these purposes—such as a toy telephone or play kitchen set.

❖ bring books to you because I want you to read them to me.

❖ begin to understand I can make things happen with my actions.

❖ learn my first few words. I repeat and practice words constantly.

❖ understand more words than I can say.

❖ say *no* quite often.

❖ make sounds like objects and animals such as cars, cats, and dogs.

❖ use gestures (pointing and reaching) to let you know what I want.

❖ can point to my body parts or other familiar objects if you ask.

❖ enjoy rhymes, word games, and songs.

From 18 to 24 months, I

❖ find objects hidden in more than one place.

❖ point out family members in photos.

❖ begin to sort objects and toys by their like and unlike qualities.

❖ copy the actions of others.

❖ can complete a simple jigsaw puzzle.

❖ learn to identify several common smells.

❖ like learning about cause-effect relationships (splashing water, banging on a drum).

❖ may search quite a while for a missing toy.

❖ know a familiar person is absent. I can point to the door and say *gone*.

❖ enjoy pretend play.

❖ may use a word too broadly or too narrowly. For instance, I may call all four-legged animals dog. I might also call my doll doll, but call all other dolls something else.

❖ can match sounds to the animals that make them.

❖ ask for food or drink when I am hungry or thirsty.

❖ may ask "What's that?" often, wanting you to name objects for me. This way, I can learn to say their names.

❖ can start a conversation with you if I want to talk.

❖ say as many as 5 to 20 words.

❖ may use my words sometimes to express frustration and anger.

❖ begin to use two words together in a sentence (*give cookie*, *big ball*, *more milk*, *my truck*, and *no shoes*).

(Continued)

From 24 to 30 months, I

❖ like to play house and imitate family life.

❖ am quite interested in children's TV shows.

❖ imitate grown-up actions such as brushing my hair or cooking dinner.

❖ can find objects that are moved out of sight.

❖ begin to sort by shape and color. For instance, I can separate all the round objects or all the red objects from a pile of toys.

❖ enjoy make-believe play. I can pretend to be someone else now.

❖ follow two-step directions. (Please pick up this toy and put it in the toy box.)

❖ look at books with you and by myself.

❖ point to objects and pictures in a book when you name them.

❖ explain to you what is happening in the pictures I have drawn.

❖ know conversation is two-way. I wait for my turn to speak.

❖ ask you many questions. Many of my questions may start with *why*.

❖ understand most of what you say now.

❖ use longer sentences than before.

❖ enjoy listening to stories and rhymes.

❖ understand the concepts *in*, *out*, and *under*, as well as *soon*, *before*, and *after*.

❖ start using the pronouns *I* and *me*.

❖ repeat words I overhear others use in conversation.

From 30 to 36 months, I

❖ start to understand relationships between objects (chair to table, hat to head).

❖ try to put three or four objects in order (smallest to biggest; shortest to longest).

❖ get more involved in my make-believe and pretend play. I love to play dress-up.

❖ listen when you explain things or give reasons.

❖ follow three-part commands.

❖ use words to indicate quantity (some, more, gone, big, little).

❖ know directions (up, down, behind, under, over).

❖ can answer simple *where* questions.

❖ combine two or more words (throw ball; get ball).

❖ change my tone of voice when asking questions.

❖ ask the names of objects and repeat your answers.

❖ improve in my use of grammar. For instance, I start to use the correct word order (subject, verb, object) in my sentences.

❖ begin making plurals by adding -*s* to the ends of words (birds, cats, cars, cookies, toys).

❖ use the pronouns *he*, *she*, *his*, *him*, and *her*.

❖ improve in my use of negative language (*no eat* becomes *I'm full*).

❖ use past tense (he bit me; I dropped ball).

❖ may be able to name several colors.

❖ can follow the story line in a book. I will remember what happens in my favorite books. In fact, I may even "read" a familiar storybook to you.

From 12 and 18 months, I

❖ show a preference for my family members over others.

❖ hand an object to you and wait for you to do what I want you to do with it.

❖ recognize when important people are missing.

❖ may offer toys to others but immediately want them back. I don't understand the concept of sharing.

❖ demand your attention much of the time.

❖ recognize myself in mirrors, pictures, and on videotape.

❖ may enjoy playing alone or beside others.

❖ know some standards of conduct.

❖ want to do things by myself. I persist at tasks I know I can do.

❖ will perform for an audience.

❖ am self-centered. I think about my own needs and wants, not the needs and wants of others.

❖ show my independence by saying *no* often. I may do just the opposite of what I'm asked to prove I can.

❖ laugh if you chase me or if I chase you.

❖ can feel embarrassment.

❖ show empathy to others.

❖ might hit people or throw things when I'm angry. Please help me learn not to do this.

❖ disagree or am stubborn at times.

❖ rely on your facial expressions, body language, and tone of voice to tell me how to behave or react in a new situation.

From 18 to 24 months, I

❖ ask for permission to do things sometimes.

❖ seek approval in social situations.

❖ like to follow older children around and do what they do.

❖ act out real-life events in my play.

❖ prefer to play alone but near others.

❖ will play among others in a group but I still don't understand sharing very well.

❖ sometimes defy my parents or other adults.

❖ want everything my own way.

❖ copy actions of others (parents, older children).

❖ test the limits of my parents and caregivers.

❖ show love to my favorite people. I smile, hug, and kiss you to show I care.

❖ may show an increasing need to have my security object with me at all times. This might be a stuffed toy, doll, or blanket.

❖ am possessive of my toys and may hide them from others.

❖ may start having new fears.

❖ start having temper tantrums.

❖ become more aware of my own feelings. In the middle of this stage, I'm just starting to learn to be concerned about others.

❖ become frustrated easily.

❖ use words to describe my emotions (love, hurt, cry).

(Continued)

Developmental Milestones: Social and Emotional Development

12 to 36 Months

From 24 to 30 months, I

* might grab a toy I want from another child's hands.
* learn rules through trial and error. When you correct me, I may try another way of doing things.
* play well with older children.
* imitate others through pretend play.
* may hand a toy to another child without being asked. I can share sometimes.
* see the world from my own point of view.
* understand the concept of friends.
* am becoming aware of my gender (being a boy or a girl).
* start to develop self-control.
* find it difficult to wait for anything.
* feel jealousy sometimes.
* may become manipulative and bossy.
* trust most adults, but especially you.
* am able to explain my desires and feelings using words and gestures.
* may have mood swings often.
* can express sadness or stress.
* show emotions of pride, guilt, and shame.
* might start to be afraid of the dark.

From 30 to 36 months, I

* can tell whether other children are boys or girls.
* know the difference between on purpose and accident.
* start to cooperate.
* play both near other children and with them.
* will say *please* and *thank you* if you remind me.
* like to hide from others.
* know what is *mine* and *hers*.
* insist on doing things for myself even if it's hard or it takes longer.
* want to be independent, but I am afraid of new experiences.
* like to dress and undress myself. Please praise me for trying.
* want to be accepted by others.
* begin to know right behavior from wrong behavior. I feel bad when I am scolded for mistakes.
* may find it hard to focus on new tasks.
* insist on being the center of attention at times.
* show negative feelings and occasional bad temper.
* show affection openly (hugs, kisses, pats).
* express a wide range of emotion.

Chapter 7
Keeping Your
Toddler Healthy
and Safe

Health is just as much a concern in the toddler years as it was in infancy. Your toddler needs regular medical checkups. He should keep getting the immunizations he needs. Taking these steps will help your child stay healthy.

Even with routine care, however, toddlers get sick from time to time. As a parent, you'll need to know how to care for your child when he is sick. This chapter will teach you how to do this. It will also explain how you can tell when it's time to call a health care provider. With practice, you can meet the special needs your child has when he is sick.

Safety is also a concern. Your toddler can do more on his own now. He still needs you to constantly supervise him, though. Your toddler has an active and curious nature. He moves quickly from place to place without checking for danger. Your child doesn't know as much about possible dangers as you do. He needs you to protect him. Accidents are a major cause of death for young children. Work with your child to keep him safe and prevent serious accidents.

Your Toddler's Medical Checkups

Routine medical checkups are essential. These checkups are often called <u>well-child exams</u>. Your toddler needs them at 12, 15, 18, 24, and 36 months. This helps her health care provider be sure she is healthy and developing properly. The provider will measure her height and weight and do a complete physical exam. The provider will ask you about her eating, sleeping, and toileting habits. At this visit, you can ask the provider any questions you might have about your toddler's health.

In addition, your toddler can receive the rest of her immunizations at these visits. These will protect her from diseases that pass easily from child to child. See Figure 7-1 for a basic immunization schedule for your toddler. Your provider can tell you exactly when it's best to have each one. For toddlers with up-to-date immunizations, vaccines will be needed at or before 18 months of age. More will be given when your child is four to six years old.

Immunization Schedule for Toddlers

Immunization	Age (in Months)		
	12	15	18
Hepatitis B*			
Diphtheria, tetanus, and pertussis (DTaP)			
Polio (IPV)			
Haemophilus influenzae type b (Hib)			
Measles, mumps, rubella (MMR)			
Chicken pox (varicella)			
*if third dose not given between 6 and 12 months			

American Academy of Pediatrics

Even though your child is a toddler, immunizations are still important. Your child's health care provider can tell you exactly when to schedule these.

Caring for a Sick Child

Caring for a sick child isn't easy! When your child is sick, it may seem like his personality changes. He may become fussy, clingy, grumpy, whiny, or short-tempered. Your child may seem very weak and low on energy. He may cry more than usual and demand your attention. This behavior is easier to take if you remember your child doesn't feel well. See Figure 7-2. Soon he will be himself again. Try to remain calm, cheerful, and confident. Your child will pick up on your attitude. If you're negative, he'll be more negative. If you act worried, he'll be scared. Being pleasant and loving will comfort your child.

Try to keep your sick toddler comfortable and occupied. He may insist on being up and about even if he isn't feeling well. Keep him busy with quiet, calm activities that can be done in bed or on the couch. Your child's rest is important, too. Spend extra time talking, reading stories, and playing simple games together. Your child needs your comfort, love, and reassurance. This extra attention makes him feel special. It can help him feel better faster.

Taking Your Child's Temperature

When your child is sick, she may have a fever (body temperature that is above the normal range). For most people, normal body temperature is 98.6°F. Some people have normal body temperatures that are a degree or two lower or higher than this. At various times of the day and at different activity levels, each person's body temperature can rise or fall a couple of degrees. This is the person's range of normal temperatures. For instance, the range of normal for one child might be from 96°F to 99°F. Anytime your child's temperature is above what is the range of normal for her, she has a fever.

Not all illnesses include a fever, but a fever is a pretty good sign that an illness is present. Fever means the body is fighting an infection. It is a sign the body is protecting itself. Before calling your child's health care provider about an illness, it's a good idea to take her temperature. Your provider will usually ask what the temperature is.

You may wonder how to take your child's temperature. You can use a digital thermometer, a mercury thermometer, or a temperature strip. Any of these methods can tell you whether your child has a fever.

7-2 When your child doesn't feel well, she may not behave as well as usual. She needs your love and attention at this time.

The digital thermometer is the preferred kind to use. It is quite accurate and very easy to use. The temperature is given in easy-to-read digital numbers. Read the instructions carefully before using this type of thermometer. Exact directions may vary from one digital thermometer to the next. A main benefit of digital thermometers is being much safer than traditional mercury thermometers.

A mercury thermometer is a thin glass tube with a band of mercury inside. The mercury expands with heat and can measure a person's temperature. The temperature is read by noting how far the mercury rose using the corresponding numbers and degree marks printed on the thermometer.

Mercury thermometers were once the only option for taking temperatures. Now, however, they are being used less and less often. This is mainly due to the health risk they pose if the glass breaks and the mercury leaks out or evaporates into the air. See Figure 7-3 for more information on the danger of mercury thermometers.

Mercury Thermometers: A Health Concern

For many years, they were the standard way to take a temperature. Now, mercury thermometers are more often being thought of as a threat. Some cities and one state have banned the sale and manufacture of mercury thermometers. Many hospitals around the country have pledged to stop using equipment containing mercury. Several top retailers have agreed to stop selling these thermometers. Why?

All these groups know mercury is highly poisonous to humans and animals when released into the air or water. In humans, exposure to mercury can affect the brain, spinal cord, kidneys, and liver. Animals can be harmed by mercury, too. In fact, several species of fish and birds have been contaminated by swimming in and drinking water that has been contaminated by mercury. This happens most often when mercury-containing equipment is thrown into a landfill and the mercury seeps into groundwater. Mercury can also be released into the air when garbage in a landfill is burned.

For this reason, never dispose of a mercury thermometer (or batteries containing mercury) by throwing them into the trash. Instead, call your area's household hazardous waste collection facility or local health department to find out where to take these items. This office will be able to dispose of them properly.

If you break a mercury thermometer in your home, remove all people and pets from the area at once. You will need to take special precautions when cleaning up the spill to protect yourself and your family. Call your state pollution control agency or local health department office for

7-3 If broken, mercury thermometers can pose a risk to the environment and your family's health.

If you have a mercury thermometer, you can use it to take your child's temperature. Be very careful not to break it, though. Start by shaking the thermometer gently until the mercury band falls below 96°F. To shake it, hold the end opposite the bulb tightly between your fingers and snap your wrist. What you will do next depends on whether you will use the rectal, armpit, or oral method.

Until your child is two years old, it is best to use the rectal or ear methods to take her temperature. Once she is two, you can start taking her temperature under her armpit. Wait to use the oral method (placing the thermometer under the tongue) until your child is six or seven years old. By this age, you can teach your child not to bite the thermometer.

Rectal Method

Rub the bulb end of the thermometer with rubbing alcohol or soap and water. Rinse in cool, clear water. Place a small amount of petroleum jelly on the bulb end. Take your child's diaper or pants off. Lay her belly-down on a firm surface. Firmly press the palm of one hand against her lower back just above the buttocks. Hold her still. Insert the lubricated thermometer ½-inch to 1-inch into the anal opening. Hold the thermometer in place for two minutes. Remove and read the thermometer. Wash the thermometer (and your hands) with soap and water after each use. Rectal temperatures are about 1°F above actual body temperatures. This means an average temperature would be 99.6°F when taken rectally.

Ear Method

Digital ear thermometers are now available. These thermometers are often quite fast and easy to use. They are also quite expensive. If you use an ear thermometer, follow the directions on the package. Exact instructions may vary from one thermometer to the next.

Armpit Method

Take your child's shirt off. Hold the thermometer under her bare armpit for three minutes. Hold her arm across her chest to keep the thermometer in place. Note that temperatures taken under the armpit are about 1°F under actual body temperature. This means an average temperature would be 97.6°F when taken under the arm.

Temperature strips are a fairly new kind of thermometer. These strips are much like stickers. They are placed on the skin for a short time (generally one to two minutes). They work by sensing body heat. This strip is marked with degree marks and numbers, much like a mercury thermometer. The temperature strip also has a light-colored line that darkens in response to heat. You can read the temperature strip by noting how far up the line the color has changed. After one use, the strip is removed and thrown away. A temperature strip may be slightly less accurate than another type of thermometer, but it can indicate whether a fever is present.

Giving Medications

When your child is sick, he may need to take some medicine. There are two main types of medicines you will give your child. A prescription medication is one that is ordered by a health care provider. You can only buy it at a pharmacy with a provider's permission.

Always read the label of the prescription. Follow the directions exactly. Give the prescribed dose for as long as it says. Unless your provider says it's okay, don't stop the medicine when your child starts to feel better. The illness might return if you stop too early. If you have any questions, ask the provider or a pharmacist. Tell the provider if your child has any side effects from the medicine.

Sometimes you might treat your child's minor illness or discomfort yourself. Suppose your child has teething pain. In this case, you may not need to take him to his health care provider. You might just treat the pain with an over-the-counter (OTC) medicine. You can buy this kind of medicine without a prescription.

Follow the dosage instructions for an OTC drug. Be sure the medicine is safe for someone your child's age. Look on the package for the drug's expiration date. You should not use a medicine after this date. If the medicine doesn't relieve your child's symptoms, call his health care provider. You can also ask the provider which OTC drug to use.

Most prescription and OTC medicines for young children come in liquid form. Liquid is easier for your toddler to swallow than a pill. He may take medicine quite well or he may resist. You might be able to talk him into taking the medicine. Offer him a favorite food or drink to take the bad taste away.

It is important to measure liquid medicines accurately. This ensures you give the child the intended amount of medicine. A household teaspoon is not a valid measuring device. You can get a measuring spoon for measuring liquids from your pharmacy or drug store. To give medicine by spoon, hold your child upright, and place spoon on his lower lip. Raise the angle of the spoon so the medicine trickles into his mouth. If your young toddler can't swallow from a spoon, use a dropper or syringe.

When using a dropper, hold your child in a reclining position. Put the dropper into the medicine bottle. Squeeze the bulb to draw the right amount of medicine into the dropper. Continue to squeeze the bulb. Place the end of the dropper in the corner of his mouth. Gently release the bulb and the medicine will go into your child's mouth.

The syringe is used much the same way. Put the syringe into the medicine bottle. While holding the tube steady, gently pull the stopper up until the tube fills with right amount of medicine. Take the syringe out of the bottle and place the open end into the corner of your child's mouth. Slowly push the stopper all the way back to the original position, releasing the medicine into his mouth.

When to Call a Health Care Provider

You may wonder which illnesses you can treat yourself and which will require the help of a health care provider. Feel free to call the provider any time you are concerned about your child's health. Even if you will treat a minor illness yourself, the provider can offer advice. See Figure 7-4. You should also call the provider when your child has any of the following symptoms:

- high fever (101°F or higher)
- pulling at her ear and screaming
- diarrhea
- unusual skin rash
- violent vomiting or vomiting lasts a long time
- refusing several feedings or eating amounts much less than usual
- lingering and rasping cough
- breathing difficulties
- injury to the head or loss of consciousness

 As a parent, it's your job to contact your child's health care provider when you have questions regarding injuries or illnesses your child has.

Childproofing Your Home

As busy as your toddler is, keeping him safe can seem impossible. It's important, though. Accidents can happen quickly. In just a few seconds' time, your toddler can get into danger. Don't underestimate his abilities. Your toddler can do many new things that lead to danger. Some examples include the following:

- opening drawers, doors, and cabinets. Your toddler can also get into storage areas and closets. Many harmful materials are stored here. Keep all unsafe items out of drawers your toddler can reach. Install child safety locks on cabinets that contain unsafe items.
- with dangerous objects. Sharp knives, forks, scissors, and electrical appliances may fascinate your toddler. They also pose a serious risk of injury. Keep these and other dangerous items out of his reach.

- ☞ climbing and moving constantly. Your toddler doesn't think about how high he can climb safely. He doesn't always know how to get down from these high places. Your toddler can't sit still for very long. You need to keep up with him to make sure he stays out of danger.

- ☞ in water. Your toddler may not have any fear of water. He also can't judge its depth. Watch your child closely when he is playing in water. See Figure 7-5.

Bonnie Mori

7-5 Your toddler may love to play in the water. Be sure to supervise her at all times, though.

Your home is full of possible dangers. All these dangers provide risks for your toddler. If you plan ahead and stay alert, you can prevent serious accidents. You can remove harmful objects and keep your child out of risky places.

Once your child is walking, you will need to childproof your entire home. Your child loves to explore new things. He touches, mouths, and tastes everything. Make your home safe for him. This will lower the chances of an accident. Learn about precautions you should take when your child is outdoors, near animals, or in the sun. Finally, be sure to watch your child constantly when you are visiting someone's home. Other families may not have taken as many safety precautions as you have.

Bedroom

Your mobile toddler spends many hours in the bedroom. Never leave her in a crib or playyard with the side down. Keep space heaters and fans out of her reach. Do not store medicines in purses or drawers in your bedroom. Your child can get into these when you're not looking. Also, put the belongings of your guests (purses, coats, and bags) out of your child's reach.

Cover all the unused electrical outlets in the home with plastic child safety caps. You can buy these at a hardware store. Tape all loose electrical cords to the wall or to the floor. This will keep your toddler from playing with them, tripping over them, or using them to pull objects down onto herself. Tie up the cords on window coverings so your child can't pull them down on herself or accidentally strangle herself with the cord. Also, be careful not to put your toddler's crib in reach of these window blind cords.

Kitchen

The kitchen is a very dangerous place for your toddler. You probably spend lots of time in this room, though. Use the following tips to promote your child's safety regarding the kitchen:

- ☞ If at all possible, keep your toddler out of the kitchen—at least while you are cooking. This will prevent many accidents. If you can't keep him out, make sure you know where he is at all times. Be sure he's not underfoot when you are walking with a hot dish or liquid.
- ☞ Always point the handles of pots and pans toward the back of the stove.
- ☞ Mop up spills from the floor immediately.
- ☞ Keep matches out of your child's reach. Install a smoke detector on every floor of your home. Keep a fire extinguisher in your kitchen, if possible.
- ☞ Unplug appliances when they are not in use (for example—crock pots, coffeemakers, toasters, blenders, and radios). This will keep your toddler from pulling them down onto himself.
- ☞ Lock sharp knives, scissors, and other sharp tools in a drawer or cabinet.
- ☞ Store breakable dishes and glasses out of your child's reach. Better yet, use plastic or unbreakable dishes until your child is older.
- ☞ Keep plastic bags out of reach. This will keep your child from putting them over his face, which can cause suffocation. Put knots in plastic bags before throwing them away.

☞ Store all cleaners in a locked cupboard high out of your child's reach. Many of these can be very harmful if they are swallowed. Don't store a poisonous product in a food or drink container. Your child may mistake it for something to eat or drink. When you're finished using a cleaning supply, be sure to put it away instead of leaving it out where your child might accidentally get to it.

Bathroom

The bathroom is full of hazards, too. To best avoid these hazards, keep your child out of this room unless an adult is with her. Install a latch or hook on the outside of the bathroom door. This way your child can't get in alone. Avoid having a lock on the inside of the door, or she might accidentally lock herself in the bathroom.

Do the following to keep your child safe in the bathroom:

☞ Keep the toilet lid closed. Your child could fall in.

☞ Stay with your child when she's taking a bath. Never leave her alone in the bathtub, not even for a second. Children can drown in even very shallow water.

☞ Use a nonslip tub mat or nonskid rubber decals on the bottom of the bathtub to prevent falls.

☞ Keep razor blades, electric razors, and clippers well out of reach. Unplug hair dryers and curling irons when not in use. Store these up high and away from your child.

☞ Don't take medicine in front of your child. Never tell your child medicine is "candy". Store medicines in a high, locked cabinet. See Figure 7-6. Flush any unused or expired medicine down the toilet. (A child can pull discarded medicines out of a trash can.)

☞ Store poisonous products in a locked cupboard or high out of your child's reach. Make sure cleaners are always out of her reach when you're using them. Put these products away after each use. Do not rely on childproof caps on medicines and cleaning supplies. Children can often learn to open these.

7-6 A large number of children are poisoned each year by getting into bathroom medicine cabinets. For this reason, choose a high, locked cabinet for storing your family's medicines.

Living Room

You and your toddler will spend a lot of time together in the living room. This is one of the safest rooms in the house. Even the living room can be a dangerous place for your toddler, though. Inspect your living room, and do the following to protect him:

- ☞ Avoid placing heavy or hot objects on low tables. Move any valuable items to a high shelf until your child is older.
- ☞ Keep all houseplants out of reach. Get rid of any plants you know to be poisonous.
- ☞ Never leave matches or lighters lying around. Never leave cigarettes, ashes, or cigarette butts where your child can reach them. These can be poisonous if eaten.
- ☞ If you have a fireplace, install a fire screen. Be sure the screen is securely fitted to the wall.

Stairways

Stairways are very inviting to your toddler. He will try to use the stairs often. Protect your toddler by doing the following:

- ☞ Install safety gates at the top and bottom of each set of stairs.
- ☞ Never leave objects lying on the stairs. Mend any loose carpet or floor covering on each step.
- ☞ Measure the gaps between posts in the banister. These should be 4 inches apart or less. Your child can get her head stuck if banisters are further apart.

Garage, Basement, and Storage Sheds

Many dangerous items are stored in garages, basements, and sheds. Keep your toddler out of these areas as much as you can. Lock away all equipment that is not being used. Mowers, power tools, and gardening tools can injure your child.

Store all chemicals in secure, locked areas. These include weed killers, painting supplies, and car care items. Store these items in their original containers. Put them away when you're done using them.

Remove the doors of any unused refrigerators or freezers. Toddlers have died when playing with or near these. They have become trapped inside and suffocated.

Outdoor Safety

Your child likes to play outdoors. Here he can run freely and explore. However, there are many dangers outdoors, too. You must keep your child from running out into the street. Other dangers include drowning, eating poisonous plants, and using an unsafe play area. Inspect your outdoor area and watch your toddler while he plays. Stay outside with him and be alert for possible dangers. Use the outdoor safety tips on the next page.

☞ Hold onto your toddler whenever you're near traffic.

☞ Don't allow him to play near a garage, driveway, or parked car.

☞ Set up fences or other barriers to make sure he stays within a safe area.

☞ Never leave your child in a wading pool alone. Empty the wading pool immediately after use. Never let him play near a pond, lake, or river alone.

☞ Cover all drains and pipes tightly.

☞ Remove any poisonous plants. Pull any mushrooms, toadstools, or other fungi as soon as they appear. Tell your child never to eat any plants or berries from the garden or yard.

☞ Check the safety of all play equipment often.

☞ Always protect your child from injury when playing outdoors. Have your child wear protective gear, such as helmets and the appropriate padding when riding tricycles and bicycles or using skates or skateboards. See Figure 7-7.

Sun Safety

Your child needs fresh air and sun. Too much sun can injure her skin, though. A toddler's skin is very delicate and burns easily. Severe sunburns in childhood can increase the risk of skin cancer later in life. Protect your child from sunburn by doing the following:

☞ Put sunscreen on your child every day, even in the winter. Use a lotion with an SPF (sun protection factor) of 15 or higher. Put the lotion on 30 minutes before going outside. Reapply every two hours while your child is outside.

7-7 To keep your child safe, insist he or she wear the proper protective gear for all outdoor activities.

☞ Keep your child in the shade as much as possible. Put a hat on her when she's outdoors.

☞ When you can, stay out of the sun between 10 a.m. and 2 p.m. This is when the sun's rays are strongest and can cause the most damage.

☞ If your child gets sunburned, put cool, wet towels on the burns. If she gets a fever or her skin blisters, call her health care provider.

Animal Safety

Your toddler is more likely to be bitten by a dog or a cat than you are. Your pet may bite your toddler if the pet feels jealous, threatened, or overly excited. To protect your toddler from animals, you can do the following:

☞ Look for a gentle pet. Older animals raised in a home with children may be a good choice. Younger pets are more often frisky. A young dog or cat may bite when being playful.

☞ Teach your child never to put his face close to the animal's face.

☞ Show your child how to handle your pet. See Figure 7-8. Don't let him tease an animal by pulling its tail or ears. Many bites happen when children play too roughly with pets.

☞ Warn your child not to take food or toys away from your pet. Teach your child not to disturb a pet who is eating or sleeping.

☞ Never leave your toddler alone with a pet. Stay nearby so you can step in if your child starts to play too roughly with the pet.

7-8 A pet can be a companion for your toddler. Teach your child to handle pets kindly and gently.

Handling Minor Injuries and Emergencies

Your busy toddler will get hurt sometimes. She will have many minor injuries that require your attention. If you know how to care for these injuries, you can offer the right kind of help. You will also know when an injury is too serious for you to handle. In this case, you can get emergency medical help for your child right away.

Treating Minor Injuries

A minor injury is one for which you can easily provide the needed care. Examples are minor cuts, scrapes, bee stings, bruises, blisters, and minor burns. These injuries can be painful for your child, but they are not life-threatening in most cases.

When your child comes to you with an injury, she needs you to stay calm. Comfort her and quickly assess the extent of the injury. Decide whether this is a minor injury you can handle or an emergency that demands immediate medical attention. To be able to make the right decision, you should know something about treating minor injuries. Figure 7-9 gives the most common minor injuries and their treatments. If you have any questions about treating a minor injury, feel free to call your child's health care provider.

Giving First Aid in an Emergency

An emergency is a situation in which your toddler needs immediate medical help. This is not a time when you can give your child all the care he needs. You will need the help of a hospital to care for your child. In an emergency, call 911 or take your child to the nearest hospital emergency room. Act quickly, because a delay may be life-threatening. Figure 7-10 lists several emergency situations that require immediate medical help.

When an emergency arises, it takes a little time to get medical help. You must either wait for an ambulance or drive to the hospital, which takes time. In many emergencies, you need to provide some care until medical help is received. The temporary care given immediately after a serious illness or injury is called first aid.

Treating Minor Injuries

If the situation allows, wash your hands with soap and warm water before attending to your child. Try to be calm and keep your child calm.

Animal Bites

1. Use direct pressure on the wound for five minutes to control any bleeding.
2. Gently wash the wound with soap and warm water.
3. Call your child's health care provider for advice. If the wound is large or still bleeding, keep applying pressure to the area while calling the provider.
4. If you can, find out whether the animal is current on its rabies shots.

Insect Bites and Stings

Mosquito, fly, flea, or bedbug bites

1. Apply calamine lotion to the bite (except near the eyes and genitals) to relieve itching.

Wasp or bee sting

1. Remove the stinger to keep more venom from entering the wound. You can do this by gently scraping across it with the blunt edge of a table knife, credit card, or your fingernail.
2. Apply a cold cloth to reduce pain and swelling.
3. Call your child's health care provider for further advice.
4. Watch for signs of an allergic reaction to the sting. These include the following: weakness, collapse, loss of consciousness; sudden difficulty breathing; hives or itching all over the body, and extreme swelling near the eye, lips, or genitals. Call 911 or take your child to the hospital immediately if your child shows these signs.

Minor Cuts and Scrapes

1. Apply pressure to the wound for five minutes. If the cut is very deep or won't stop bleeding, take your child to a hospital immediately. He may need stitches to close the wound.
2. If the wound is not serious and the bleeding stops, run cold water over the wounded areas and wash thoroughly with soap.
3. Gently pat dry with a clean cloth.
4. Apply an antiseptic cream.
5. Cover with an adhesive bandage.

Blisters

1. Cover the blister with a clean, dry dressing (not an adhesive bandage).
2. Do not break a blister. In a day or two, the body will absorb the fluid inside. The blistered skin will dry and peel.

Bruises

1. If the bruise is large, apply a cold compress for about half an hour to reduce the pain.
2. If the pain gets worse within 24 hours, call your health care provider. This may indicate a fracture.

Object Stuck in the Nose or Ear

1. Tell your child to breathe through her mouth.
2. Do not try to remove the object. Doing so might cause injury or push the object in further.
3. Take your child to the hospital right away to have the object removed.

(Continued)

7-9 Minor injuries are common among toddlers. Knowing how to treat these when they occur helps you not to panic.

Treating Minor Injuries

Nosebleeds

1. Have your child tilt his head forward a little.

2. Use a clean cloth to apply slight pressure to the nostril where the bleeding is occurring. Keep applying this pressure for a few minutes.

3. If bleeding continues, call 911 or take your child to the hospital.

Bump on Head

1. If the scalp is bleeding, apply firm, steady pressure with a sterile gauze pad for 10 minutes or until the bleeding stops. If bleeding won't stop, call 911 or take your child to the hospital.

2. Watch for signs of a concussion. Call your health care provider or 911 if your child is unconscious, vomits, or is drowsy and cranky. Let your health care provider know if your child complains of a headache that won't go away.

Burns

Deep or serious burns

1. Do not try to provide care yourself. Call 911 or rush your child to the hospital. Don't apply ice or water to the burn. Don't try to remove burned clothing from the skin.

Minor burns

1. Use an ice pack on the burn to relieve the pain and swelling.

2. Cover the burn with a clean, dry gauze pad.

Splinters

Glass or fiberglass splinters

1. Don't try to remove the splinter yourself. Have a health care provider remove it.

Wood splinters

1. If you can see the end of the splinter, use sterilized tweezers to pull the splinter out gently. (To sterilize the tweezers, hold them over an open flame for a few seconds. Then allow them to cool.) Pull the splinter out in the same direction it went in.

2. After removing the splinter, squeeze the area to make it bleed a little. This will help cleanse the wound.

3. Wash the area with soap and warm water.

4. Apply an antiseptic cream.

7-9 *(Continued)*

Some types of first aid are easy to provide. For instance, you can try to stop heavy bleeding by applying pressure to a wound with a clean cloth. This does not require special training. Other types of first aid are more difficult to learn. Two examples are cardiopulmonary resuscitation (CPR) and mouth-to-mouth resuscitation.

Emergencies Requiring Immediate Medical Help

❖ electric shock

❖ poisoning or suspected poisoning

❖ burn or scald larger than your child's hand

❖ severe bleeding from a wound

❖ any injury to the eyes or ears

❖ contact with an acid or burning chemical

❖ unconsciousness

❖ pale blue or gray skin around the lips or under the fingernails

❖ possible broken bone or sprain

 Some emergencies require immediate medical help. If any of these occur, take your child to a hospital at once or call 911 for an ambulance.

To learn these techniques, you need to take special first aid classes. Trying to give this type of first aid without training can result in serious injury or death.

Taking first aid classes is a good idea for parents. This prepares them to give more complicated types of first aid if needed. Being able to provide this care in an emergency can save someone's life. You can take first aid classes offered by your community or the local Red Cross.

Accidents happen suddenly, and they require fast action. You have to be ready to handle accidents when they occur. If you stay calm, it will help you comfort your child. Try to stay in control of your emotions. Your child needs your emotional support. Think quickly and assess the situation. Then decide what action to take. In many emergencies, following the basic first-aid steps given in Figure 7-11 will help.

Two types of emergencies are very common among toddlers. These are choking and poisoning. If your child is choking or appears to have been poisoned, it is important to act quickly. The following sections describe first aid you can give if choking or poisoning occurs.

Choking

Choking kills many toddlers each year. Your toddler may choke on food or small objects she puts in her mouth. These can get stuck in her mouth or throat, blocking her airways. When someone is choking, at first they may try to cough the object out. If your child can cough, speak, or cry, she doesn't need you to do anything. Just stand by with a watchful eye. Her body is trying to handle the problem on its own.

Your child is in danger if she loses her ability to cough, speak, breathe, or cry. Another sign is that her lips and the beds of her fingernails might begin to turn blue. At this point, your child needs your help immediately.

To help your choking toddler, use the abdominal thrust, or Heimlich maneuver. This first-aid technique can remove an object stuck in the throat or windpipe. Use this only if your child is conscious (awake) but cannot speak or cough. Follow the steps on the next page.

Basic First-Aid Steps to Use in an Emergency

Use the following guidelines for basic first aid in an emergency:

❖ Act quickly and calmly. Find out whether the person is breathing and/or conscious (awake). Make sure the injured person has nothing in his mouth or throat. Clear the throat of any food or other items.

❖ Stop any bleeding. Apply pressure to the wound with a clean cloth or dressing. Lay your child down. Keep the injured part of the body in a position above the heart to slow the flow of blood to the wound. Do not use a tourniquet to stop the bleeding. The incorrect use of a tourniquet can cause even more injuries.

❖ Ask someone to call for medical help. Stay with the injured person until help arrives.

❖ Try to prevent shock. Keep the injured person warm. Keep the injured person lying down.

❖ Remain calm. Move the injured person only if there is an immediate threat of further injury if he or she is not moved. Moving an injured person may cause even more injury.

7-11 Learning these basic first-aid steps can help you provide the right kind of care in an emergency situation.

1. Stand behind your child and use your hand to form a fist. Press the thumb of this fist on top of your child's navel.

2. Cup your other hand over this fist. Keep your elbows out and away from your child. Do not squeeze with your arms.

3. Press in and up with one firm motion. Repeat until the object comes out.

4. If this doesn't work after a few tries, call 911. Continue to repeat the steps until medical help arrives.

Poisoning

Toddlers are also at high risk for poisoning accidents. Your toddler is curious about everything. He explores new things by touching and tasting them. As you know, not all objects or substances are safe to touch and taste. Your toddler may not understand this, though. This is one reason you must keep an eye on him at all times. Watch for signs of possible poisoning. Finding your child with an open or empty container of a poisonous item is a warning sign. See Figure 7-12 for other possible signs of poisoning.

Poison can be dangerous if it comes into contact with your child's mouth, eyes, or skin. If the poison is in his eyes, gently wash them with plenty of tap water for at least 15 minutes. Have your child keep his eyes open during this time. If your child gets poison on his skin, wash with large amounts of lukewarm water. Remove any poison-soaked clothing.

Possible Signs of Poisoning

Many children are accidentally poisoned each year. Signs that may indicate poisoning include the following:

❖ burns on the lips or mouth
❖ fresh stains on clothing
❖ unusual drool or odd-smelling breath
❖ sudden behavior changes, such as being sleepy, jumpy, or out of sorts
❖ burns or rashes on the skin
❖ irritated eyes
❖ choking, coughing, nausea, convulsions, or dizziness

 7-12 Being familiar with the warning signs of poisoning can help you recognize them quickly if an emergency arises.

Providing Help for Poisoning Victims. **If you think your child has swallowed a poison, look into his mouth. Remove any remaining poison. Check for burns, cuts, odors, or unusual coloring. Try to figure out what was swallowed. Keep any containers you find. If your child vomits and you don't know what was eaten, keep a sample of the vomit. This can help the hospital determine what the poison is.**

If you find your child unconscious and you suspect poisoning, call 911 for immediate assistance or take your child to the nearest emergency room. If you have the poison's container, take it to the hospital with you.

If your child is awake, call his health care provider or your local Poison Control Center right away. Time is very important. Even if he appears to be fine, your child may need some kind of treatment. When you call, you will be asked your child's name, age, and weight. Tell the person what poison you think was swallowed and an approximate time. If you know what the poison was, take the container to the phone with you when you call. Read the label off its container to the Poison Control Center operator. Estimate how much poison was swallowed if you can.

The Poison Control Center or your child's provider may tell you to cause your child to vomit. This will quickly get the poison out of his stomach. To induce (cause) vomiting, you would use the recommended amount of syrup of ipecac. This is an over-the-counter medicine. You can buy it at a pharmacy. (You should keep syrup of ipecac on hand for possible poisoning emergencies.) With the syrup of ipecac, you can give your child a few ounces of water or favorite drink. If he has not vomited within 20 minutes, give another dose of syrup of ipecac and more fluids.

Not all cases call for vomiting, however. <u>Never</u> cause vomiting unless directed to do so by a doctor or Poison Control Center. In some cases, causing your child to vomit a poison can be dangerous. This is true if the child is unconscious or having a convulsion or seizure. In these conditions, a child might choke if caused to vomit.

Another time not to induce vomiting is if a child has swallowed chemicals or a product containing petroleum. (You can tell if a product contains petroleum by checking its label.) Some of these

products can cause severe mouth and throat burns if swallowed. Vomiting the product up would burn the child's mouth and throat again on the way out of the body. This could cause even more serious injury.

In an emergency situation, knowing what to do can make the difference between panicking and helping. The same is also true when treating minor injuries. Your goal in either case is to get your child the care he needs. Learn all you can and be confident in your ability to help.

☞ Most toddlers need five routine medical checkups. At these checkups, toddlers can receive immunizations to protect them against childhood diseases. Parents can also ask questions about their child's health.

☞ Caring for a sick child involves giving comfort and extra attention. Check your child's temperature before calling her health care provider. Give medications exactly as directed by her provider. Learn what symptoms mean you should call the provider right away.

☞ Since your toddler is active and busy, you must childproof your entire home for his safety. This takes planning and a watchful eye, but it's important.

☞ Kitchens and bathrooms are the most dangerous rooms for your toddler. Don't allow her to be in these rooms without an adult present. Lock away all cleaners, medicines, and poisonous items. Keep other dangerous items out of reach.

☞ The bedroom, living room, and stairways can also be dangerous for your toddler. Look for possible risks as you make these rooms safe for him. Use gates on stairways, covers on electrical outlets, and a fire screen on fireplaces.

☞ Keep your basement, garage, and storage sheds locked when you're not using them. This will keep your curious toddler out of danger in these areas. In addition, unplug power equipment and lock dangerous materials away.

☞ Outdoor dangers include drowning, eating poisonous plants, using unsafe play areas, being hurt by an animal, getting a sunburn, and running into the street. Your constant supervision is required.

☛ If your toddler is hurt, stay calm and quickly assess the situation. Decide whether it is a minor injury you can handle or an emergency that requires immediate medical help. Learning how to treat minor injuries can be very helpful.

☛ In an emergency situation, you may need to provide first aid until medical help arrives. Taking a first aid class can teach you how to provide lifesaving aid. You can also learn basic first-aid steps. Choking and poisoning are common emergencies among toddlers.

Chapter 8
Guiding Your
Young Child

Your child is not born knowing how you expect her to behave. She learns from her experiences. As a parent, you will guide and shape your child's behavior. One of your goals may be to correct and prevent misbehavior. This can be challenging, but it is important. Your child relies on you to teach her what behaviors are acceptable in our society. In this chapter, you will learn about guidance and discipline and their role in shaping behavior.

Understanding Young Children

If you know what young children are like, you will have an easier time guiding their behavior. The following paragraphs describe a few common behavior patterns.

☞ A young child mainly thinks about himself and what is his. Only as he gets older can he start thinking about other members of the family. This is not a selfish act or one he chooses. At this young age, his mind just doesn't work that way. He can't yet see a situation from someone else's point of view.

☞ A young child is just a beginner. Your child is just learning, and he makes a lot of mistakes. He still has plenty of time to learn from his mistakes, though. Understand that many of his skills are not perfected—he still needs lots of practice and praise.

☞ A young child has a short memory. Although his memory is growing fast, your toddler still can't remember much. He often forgets directions. Repeat them, using simple words. You'll have to remind your child over and over again what he should do. See Figure 8-1. Use gentle reminders and a friendly tone of voice.

☛ A young child is not good at sitting still. Don't expect a toddler to sit quietly in one place for very long. This is hard for him to do. Give him toys or books to keep him occupied if he must sit and wait a while.

☛ A young child is not good at being quiet. Your toddler makes lots of sounds, and his play is noisy. Don't expect him to be quiet all the time. This is asking too much of him.

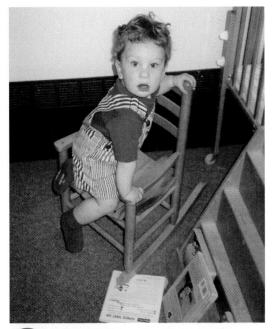

In trying to understand your young child, you may wonder why he misbehaves. If you know what the problem is, you might be able to respond more effectively.

 Young children forget instructions easily. You'll have to remind your child often that chairs are for sitting.

How Your Child Learns Behavior

As a parent, it's your job to help your child learn appropriate behavior. You also want her to avoid using negative behavior. To influence your child's behavior, you need to understand how this behavior is learned. Four important ways are imitation, direct teaching, trial and error, and reinforcement.

Imitation

Your child learns by imitating, or copying the actions of, other people. He constantly watches what others say and do. Your child might imitate the look on your face or your body language. He will use many of the words he hears others using. You will see this imitation in everyday life as well as in your child's play. At times, you will find this imitation cute. Other times, you may be less pleased.

Keep in mind your child will imitate negative behaviors just as quickly as he copies positive ones. At this age, he depends on you; he can't tell the difference between right and wrong on his own. It may surprise you how quickly he picks up habits such as cursing, yelling, and complaining. If you protect your child from these negative examples, he will learn more positive ones. If someone else is setting a bad example for your child, think about what you might do to change this.

Your child imitates the people in his life. They are his role models. A role model is a person whose actions are imitated by others. As a parent, you are your child's first and most important role model. You're the person he looks up to most. He will learn much of his behavior from imitating you. Your child will treat others in the same way you do. He will behave as you do in many situations.

Other people will serve as role models, too. Your child may pick up the actions and attitudes of family members, caregivers, and friends. If people around your child are setting a poor example, it's your job to explain to them in a respectful way how their behavior affects your child. Limit his contact with these people if they choose not to change their behavior.

Young children also imitate characters they see on TV shows and cartoons, in the movies, and in other media sources. These can be role models as well. Many studies show a very strong link between exposure to violent media and aggressive behaviors. Limits your child's exposure to media may be wise. In fact, the American Academy of Pediatrics strongly recommends avoiding TV viewing for children under age two, and limiting the exposure of older children to two hours or less daily.

Your child looks to his role models for an example. Be sure the examples he sees are good ones. As his most important role model, you need to behave appropriately. You're responsible for using the kind of behavior you want him to imitate.

Direct Teaching

Children learn much through direct teaching, or giving clear instructions on how to do something. For instance, your child learns to brush her teeth because you have shown her how to do it. You and other adults often use this method with your child. When you use direct teaching, remember to be patient with your child. She needs time to practice her new skills. Praise her for her efforts.

Trial and Error

A third way of learning is by trial and error. Trial and error means trying something in new ways until finding a way that works. In this method, your child teaches himself by experimenting. He learns from his mistakes. When he finds a solution, he will repeat it. See Figure 8-2. For example, your child may attempt to open a box. It may take him many tries before he succeeds. Once he learns a way to open the box, he will try to open similar boxes in this same way.

 This boy is using trial and error as he solves the puzzle. He keeps trying new ways to fit the pieces in until he finds a way that works.

Reinforcement

You can shape your child's behavior by the way you respond to it. Your response to her behavior is known as reinforcement. Your response can encourage your child to repeat a behavior. You could also respond in a way that discourages her from repeating a behavior.

Rewards are one type of reinforcement. Praise, attention, privileges, and other rewards increase the chance that a behavior will occur again. For instance, thanking your child for a certain behavior encourages her to repeat it. By praising your child when she behaves well, you will encourage her to behave this way more often.

You can also reinforce an undesired behavior if you reward it. Suppose your child gets out of bed every night. Do you let her cuddle with you and watch TV when she does this? If so, you are rewarding her with your attention and special privileges. You're making it more likely she will keep getting out of bed every night. Leading her back to her bed in a firm but friendly manner does not encourage this behavior to continue.

Your child is less likely to repeat behaviors that get a negative response. Your child will be less likely to repeat behavior that results in punishment, correction, disapproval, or removal of privileges. Suppose your child calls another child names. If you show your disapproval of this behavior, she will soon stop doing it. On the other hand, if you laugh at the behavior, your child may keep calling people names.

Think carefully about your response to your child's behavior. Which behaviors are you reinforcing? Are these the ones you want her to keep using? Are there other desired behaviors you could encourage in this way? Are there other undesired behaviors you could discourage? Looking at your role in your child's behavior can be helpful. This way you can change your response to her behavior when needed to influence her behavior.

The Importance of Self-Esteem

As you guide your child, one of your goals should be to enhance his self-esteem. Self-esteem is the feeling of confidence and satisfaction a person has with himself. Your child needs a sense of self-esteem. He needs to feel he has worth and value. Your child's level of self-esteem is based on how he thinks and feels about himself. If he feels very good about himself, he has a high amount of self-esteem.

A child with self-esteem likes himself and is more likely to behave in acceptable ways. He feels confident in himself and his abilities. He tries hard when faced with a challenge. This child believes he can do almost anything if he just tries hard enough.

Children with high amounts of self-esteem have a "can do" approach to life. These children set goals for themselves and work to achieve those goals. They don't give up easily. Having self-esteem is a key element of their success.

On the other hand, a child who lacks self-esteem may feel unimportant and unworthy. This child is more likely to misbehave. He feels frustrated and powerless. He lacks confidence in his abilities. A child with little self-esteem may give up quickly when faced with a challenge. He has learned to be helpless. This child often says <u>I don't know how</u>, <u>I can't</u>, and <u>Do it for me</u>.

As a parent, you play an important role in building your child's self-esteem. Being warm and nurturing toward your child will help him feel he is loved. It will give him a sense of belonging. He needs to know he matters to you. Children who feel loved are more likely to develop a sense of self-esteem. See Figure 8-3.

 When your child knows you love him, it will show in his sense of self-esteem.

As your child learns new skills and behaviors, compliment him on both big and small successes. This helps boost his confidence. Encourage him to keep trying at difficult tasks you know he's capable of doing. Tell him you know he can do it. However, avoid pushing your child too hard. Pushing a child to develop new skills before he is ready can make him feel inadequate. It might lower his confidence.

Your child's self-esteem starts with his early home life. It continues to form throughout childhood. People with high amounts of self-esteem tend to achieve better in school, personal relationships, and the workplace.

Guidance and Discipline

Guidance means directing, supervising, and influencing your child's behavior. It includes every way in which you shape her actions. You may not even know all the effects you have on her behavior. Some effects are intentional, while others are not. Guidance can be either direct or indirect.

Helping your child use appropriate behavior is the main goal of guidance. Much of guidance deals with preventing misbehavior. You'll have to monitor your child's actions until she learns self-control. Being able to regulate her own behavior is a result of proper guidance.

Suppose your child is standing on a chair. An example of guidance would be telling her, "Chairs are for sitting." In this way, you have influenced your child to change her behavior. You have let her know what to do instead. In this case, you would continue to watch closely. If she still doesn't sit, help her to do so or remove her from the chair. Supervision is a big part of guidance.

Discipline is the process of teaching and training your child to behave in acceptable ways. It is a part of guidance. Discipline includes every way in which you choose to teach or train her. The goal of discipline is to teach her about acceptable and unacceptable behavior. Much of discipline deals with correcting your child's misbehavior. As a result of proper discipline, she will learn self-control and form a conscience.

Suppose your child refuses to hold your hand when walking on a busy sidewalk. An example of discipline would be reminding your child of the rules and their consequences. You might say, "We have to hold hands while we're walking. If you won't hold my hand, I will have to carry you to keep you safe." Part of discipline is following through with the consequences every time your child chooses to misbehave.

You will guide and discipline your child until she reaches adulthood. As she grows, you will need to adjust the methods you use. Methods that work well for infants are not always as useful for older children. If you provide the proper guidance and discipline, your child will behave even when you're not around. She will become an adult who can control her own behavior and tell right from wrong.

You can guide your child's behavior in two major ways. These are indirect guidance and direct guidance.

Indirect Guidance

Indirect guidance means setting up your child's surroundings to encourage good behavior. In this way, indirect guidance can help you prevent misbehavior. These are steps you can take ahead of time to help your child.

Childproof Your Home

Childproofing means making your home safe for your child. This allows him to freely move about and learn through exploring. Childproofing means removing unsafe items from your child's path. It also means providing safe toys and equipment for him to explore. By removing dangers early, you are taking away temptations. You may also prevent many direct clashes with your child. With fewer chances for him to get into trouble, you may not need to correct him as often. (For more information about childproofing, see Chapters 4 and 7.)

Follow a Routine

A second helpful method is organizing your child's day into a routine. If your child knows what to expect, he feels more secure. Routines make days more pleasant and easier for both you and your child. Your routine will be unique to your family. You know your child best. You can set mealtimes around your child's hunger and sleep times around his sleep needs. See Figure 8-4 for an example of a daily routine for an infant. Be sure your routine also allows for some flexibility. Having a schedule that is too rigid can also be hard on your child.

Plan Activities for Your Child

You can also indirectly shape your child's behavior by planning activities for him to do. When you keep your child busy with many interesting things, he is less likely to misbehave. Remember he has a short attention span. Plan a number of activities for him, as well as a few backup activities. Provide items to play with that suit his age and interests. Rotate his toys so he doesn't become bored with them. For instance, store some toys out of sight for a couple of weeks. This will make the toys seem like new when you get them out again. The better you can plan ahead, the fewer conflicts you will have with your child.

Suzie's Daily Routine

3:00 a.m.	Suzie wakes up crying. She gets a diaper change, eats, and rocks with Mom for a few minutes. Then she goes back to sleep.
6:05 a.m.	Suzie wakes up crying. She gets her clothes and diaper changed, eats, and sits in her swing for half an hour.
7:45 a.m.	Mom and Suzie leave the house and get on the bus. Suzie falls asleep. Mom goes to school and Suzie goes to child care.
8:43 a.m.	Suzie wakes up, has a diaper change, and eats. The child care worker holds Suzie and plays with her.
9:57 a.m.	Suzie sits in the bouncer seat and watches the other children play. She soon falls asleep.
11:14 a.m.	Suzie has a diaper change and eats. She falls asleep again.
2:26 p.m.	Suzie wakes up, has a diaper change, and eats. The child care worker holds Suzie and plays with her.
3:40 p.m.	Mom is out of school and picks Suzie up. They ride the bus together to go home. Suzie falls asleep on the bus again.
4:20 p.m.	Mom and Suzie arrive at home. Suzie has a diaper change and takes a short nap.
5:48 p.m.	Suzie wakes up, has a diaper change, and eats. She and Mom play for a while.
7:00 p.m.	Suzie has a bath and Mom dresses her for bed. Mom reads to Suzie, rocks her, and sings a bedtime song.
8:21 p.m.	Suzie eats. Mom puts Suzie to bed.
12:00 a.m.	Suzie wakes up crying and wants to be fed. She eats and goes back to sleep.

8-4 At almost three months old, Suzie's activities start to have a pattern. Her mom uses a schedule most of the time because she knows it will give Suzie a sense of security.

Direct Guidance

Direct guidance includes all the actions and words you use to shape your child's behavior. This type of guidance helps her develop self-discipline. It involves both verbal and nonverbal acts between you and your child. Direct guidance works well with young children. A few basic techniques are described here.

Give Reminders

When your child forgets a rule, remind her again in a positive tone of voice. Explain what will happen if she doesn't follow the rule. Suppose the rule is to walk in the house and your child forgets. You might say, "The rule is to walk inside."

Follow Through with Consequences

If a rule is not followed, be sure to follow through with the stated consequence. If you don't, it can lead your child to not believe what you say. This can cause her to stop listening to you.

For example, a parent might say, "Angela, the rule is to sit in the grocery cart when we are in the store. Otherwise, we will have to go home." If Angela chooses not to sit, her parents will need to leave the store. This may not be what they wanted to do, but it is effective. If Angela's parents always respond in this way, she will soon learn to sit in the grocery cart.

Make Your No Count

When and how you say no is important. You don't want your no to lose its power by being overused. Save no for situations involving immediate safety. Call your child's name to be sure you have her attention. Then look her in the eye and say no calmly and firmly. Your serious tone of voice and facial expression will let her know she needs to stop what she's doing immediately to avoid danger. For other situations, rephrase your no as a direction for the behavior you want. For example, if you want your child to stop standing on a chair, you can tell her, "Sit in the chair."

Help with Frustrating Tasks

When your child has become so frustrated she is about to lose control, ask if you can help. Don't take over—give her just enough help to solve the problem. Offer verbal encouragement as well. This can prevent an outburst or tantrum.

Distract and Redirect Your Child

Getting your child's attention off something is called distraction. Shifting her attention from misbehavior to a new activity is called redirecting. Suppose your child is starting to get into a place she should not be. You can distract and redirect her by asking her to work on a puzzle or sing a song with you.

Offer Substitutes

If you must take something away from your child, offer her a substitute. Suppose your child has an object you don't want her to have. Trade it for an item that's acceptable. For instance, take a sharp object from her and replace it with a safe one. When your child is young, you can do this easily without her noticing you have taken the sharp object away. Once she's older, you will want to talk to her about the trade that needs to happen.

Remove

Gently remove your child from a situation when she is losing self-control. This is a good idea when the situation is dangerous. If your child is trying to hurt herself or others, taking her to another room to calm down can help. The same is true if she is trying to destroy property. Once your child regains her self-control, talk to her briefly about what happened.

Restrain

If your child is in a rage and out-of-control, gently hold her. This keeps her from hurting anyone. Speak in a calm, reassuring voice. Release her when the out-of-control behavior stops.

Ignore

If your child misbehaves for attention, ignore her. (Make sure she's safe, though.) When her misbehavior doesn't get your attention, she'll stop what she is doing. Give your child extra attention at a time when she's behaving well.

Use Positive Statements

When directing your child, give clear, simple directions. Your goal is to tell your child what you want her to do. You can do this by using positive statements. Avoid statements that tell her what not to do. These negative statements don't teach your child what to do instead. See Figure 8-5 for examples of positive versus negative statements.

Using Positive Words to Guide Your Child

Positive	Negative
Put your shirt in the hamper.	Don't throw your shirt on the floor.
Use your spoon, please.	Don't drink from your bowl.
Use your indoor voice.	Stop yelling.
Walk in the house, please.	Don't run in the house.
Take turns playing with the doll.	Don't fight over the doll.
Chairs are for sitting.	Don't stand on your chair.
Give me the cup, please.	Stop banging your cup on the table.
Pet the cat gently.	Stop pulling the cat's fur.

8-5 With practice, you can easily turn negative statements into positive ones. What other examples can you think of?

Use Eye Contact and Get on Your Child's Level

Kneel down so you can look your child in the eye. This helps get and hold her attention. It is also a sign of respect for your child. Use simple words and short sentences. Your child can see your facial expressions. This also helps her understand your message. When giving directions, call your child by her name. When she stops what she's doing to look at you, you have her full attention. Now you can tell her the directions.

Be Timely

Give your child simple directions right before you want her to do something. If you tell her too far ahead of time, she will forget. She has a short memory. Remember, your toddler can only do one thing at a time.

Warn Your Child of Upcoming Changes

Get into the habit of announcing changes in activity. For instance, give your child a warning about five minutes before it is time for bed, dinner, or play. Your warning allows her time to finish what she is doing. It also tells her what is coming next. This helps her make the transition from one activity to another more smoothly.

Guidance Changes as Your Child Grows

As your child grows, his behavior will change. The ways in which you guide him will change, too. At certain stages of development, he may be more of a challenge for you.

Infants

From birth to 12 months of age, your baby has many needs. He must be fed, diapered, and comforted whenever he demands it. This can make you, the parent, very tired. Children this age may use the following behaviors that may upset parents:

- ☞ crying for long periods of time for no apparent reason
- ☞ making messes
- ☞ exploring everything around them and getting into things
- ☞ putting things into their mouths
- ☞ expressing anger and frustration (age 12 months)
- ☞ ignoring parental requests

Most of these behaviors are to be expected from your infant. They fit his stage of development. That doesn't mean they will not frustrate you. This is normal, too.

Respond quickly to your baby. The more quickly you respond, the happier your baby will be. This makes him much easier to live with. He will feel more secure in your love for him. Your infant needs to develop this sense of security—it's a big part of his social development.

With infants, most of your guidance should be indirect. You can prevent many problems by making it easier for your baby to behave. It is easy to redirect your infant's interest to something else if need be. Offering substitutes works well, too. If you don't want him to play with the object he has, switch it for a safer one.

12 Months to 2 ½ Years

Your toddler is now starting to talk, walk, run, and climb. She is becoming more independent. As your toddler asserts this independence, you will find your child is not always agreeable. See Figure 8-6. She knows she's her own person separate from you. At this age, you may be bothered by the following behaviors:

- ☞ refusing to hold your hand in dangerous situations
- ☞ being defiant or saying no when told to do something
- ☞ not sharing or taking turns
- ☞ moving slowly or not coming when called
- ☞ wanting to have things her own way, such as routines, food, a favorite toy, or blanket
- ☞ having temper tantrums

 8-6 Your toddler has his own moods—he's not always the cheerful child you prefer.

It will help if you have a regular daily routine. Your toddler needs a schedule for eating, napping, sleeping, active play, and quiet play. This indirect guidance will help her know what to expect.

Use simple words and short sentences when you talk to your child. Be specific and direct. Saying, "Clean up this mess" is less specific than saying, "Put your books on the shelf, please." A specific, direct request leaves your child with no question what you want her to do.

Don't expect your toddler to do everything you ask, though. Demanding she obey your every command will just lead to frustration for you and your child. Pick your battles. Some behavior should simply be ignored.

Save commands for serious matters that require your child to listen. When giving her directions, try to phrase many of these as requests or questions. Children respond better to a polite, friendly voice than a loud, stern one. Instead of saying, "Pick up the blocks," you might say, "Mommy wants you to put the blocks away now." You could also say, "Let's put the blocks away. I'll help you." A third idea would be asking, "Can you put your blocks in the box?"

Be careful about asking questions or offering choices when there is no choice to be made. If you ask, "Are you ready to go to bed now," be prepared for your child to say no. She may not feel she's ready to go to bed. If you have decided it's bedtime, use a different approach. You could say, "It's bedtime now. Which pajamas do you want to wear?" When you ask her questions, be sure her honest input matters and you can accept whatever answer she gives.

Be patient. Don't push your toddler too hard. She will develop skills such as toilet learning and eating with utensils when she is ready. Praise her efforts when she makes even a little progress.

Don't try to change the behavior or take away the objects that comfort your child. A favorite pacifier or blanket helps your child feel better. She will wean herself from the comfort object when she is ready.

When your child refuses to do something, use distraction. Distraction works because children this age have a short attention span. Most children will quickly do what you want after the distraction. If your child refuses to let you put on her shoes, point to something interesting outside the window. Then go back to putting on the shoes. She may forget all about the problem and slip them right on.

2½ to 4 Years

At this age, your young child is even more independent. Most of the time, he insists on doing things for himself. Sometimes, though, he wants you to do things for him. This can lead to power struggles between the two of you. Going to the store, restaurants, and other public places can be difficult with a child of this age.

Behaviors of your older toddler that may frustrate you include the following:

- temper tantrums
- whining
- not sharing or playing well with others
- being jealous of anyone else who gets your attention
- interrupting
- not listening or following directions
- not picking up after himself
- becoming upset when he can't quite do something he wants to do
- keeping you waiting while he insists on doing something himself
- refusing to do something he normally does for himself

At this age, your child is eager to please you. See Figure 8-7. When he knows his behavior is pleasing to you, he feels happy. This is one reason praise is effective. When used carefully, your disapproval can motivate him to change. Always be sure your child knows you disapprove of his <u>behavior</u>, not of him as a person. Say, "I love you very much, but I need you to do (desired behavior) instead of (undesired behavior) next time." Otherwise, your child might think your anger means you don't love him.

Expect conflicts. They are normal with children of this age. When your child seems stuck or locked into a behavior, use distraction. Change the topic, tell him something nice, or whisper. This gets his attention off the conflict so you can move on to something else.

Esther Jacome

 8-7   his four-year-old enjoys making her parents happy. Praise helps strengthen her good behavior.

Guidelines for Effective Discipline

There are many ways to discipline a child. Not all of them work equally well, though. You may wonder how you can be effective when using discipline. Two key guidelines are to be consistent and set reasonable limits. These tips will help you use discipline effectively.

Be Consistent

Consistency means responding to a situation in the same way every time it occurs. Consistency means you always stand by your rules. Every time a rule is broken, you should respond in the same way. If you do not, the rule is meaningless to your child.

Your child will feel safer and more secure if you are consistent with her. She soon learns to predict how you will act. Neither of you will have to spend a lot of time or energy trying to figure out what you'll do next.

Consistency also means maintaining a common front. This means parents and caregivers should agree on discipline and expectations of the child. If they disagree, they should do it in private, not in front of the child. Otherwise, she may become confused and feel unsure about what her parents and caregivers expect.

Set Reasonable Limits

Limits are the rules you set for your child. These are the boundaries of what is suitable behavior for your child and what is not. Setting limits tells your child you care about him, his behavior, and his safety. Limits protect your child.

Limits are most effective for children ages three years and older. By this time, children can remember rules and can understand the reasons for them. The following are three main kinds of limits:

- ☛ protection from physical harm. You keep your child away from a hot stove. It's a rule he must hold your hand when walking along a busy street.
- ☛ protection of property. You insist for your child to return toys and clothing to their proper places. You urge him to play with a toy properly instead of banging it on the chair.

☞ protection from emotional harm. You help your child learn to deal with anger and solve conflicts with respectful words—not hitting, biting, teasing, or swearing.

Your child wants and needs limits. He doesn't have the experience to know what to do. Limits help him learn what behavior is acceptable and safe.

Make only a few rules. Starting with a small number of limits makes it easier for your child to remember them. Focus on the few rules you believe are most important. As he learns these rules, you can set one or two more.

State your limits clearly and positively. Use simple words your child understands. A clear limit tells him what is expected and when. Tell your child, "When playing outside, you must stay in the yard." This is more clear than saying, "Don't play in the street." Also, you must be consistent in enforcing limits or they won't work.

You will also need to evaluate your limits from time to time. As your child grows, some of your rules may no longer be needed. Instead, new rules may be needed to protect him. Some questions you can ask yourself when evaluating the limits you've set are listed in Figure 8-8.

Evaluating Limits

When examining your limits, ask yourself the following questions about each limit:

❖ Is this limit really important? Why?

❖ Is it clear enough for my child to understand?

❖ Does it tell my child specifically what I want him to do?

❖ Is the limit appropriate for my child developmentally?

❖ Do I (and my child's other caregivers) enforce this limit consistently?

8-8   When you're taking a look at the rules you've set, use these questions to decide whether the limits are needed.

Discipline Techniques

For discipline to work, you must use it soon after misbehavior occurs. If you wait too long, your child may forget why she's being disciplined. Young children have short memories. Remember, you're trying to teach your child which behaviors are acceptable and which are not.

Using Time-Out

Time-out means placing a child who has misbehaved in a quiet place for a few minutes. After he calms down, you can briefly talk about the problem. As a parent, your goals for using a time-out include the following:

- ☞ allowing your child to settle down
- ☞ correcting his behavior
- ☞ showing your child you care about him, but want him to keep himself in control
- ☞ stopping aggressive behavior, such as pushing, hitting, or biting
- ☞ giving yourself a short break before you talk with your child. Parents need time-outs, too.

When can you start using time-outs? Your child must first be able to understand the ideas of being quiet and waiting. This method isn't appropriate until he is at least 2 ½ years old.

Use a time-out when your child is fighting, noisy, or refusing to listen. A time-out gives everyone a chance to calm down. It is a cooling-off period. Time-out creates a physical distance between the child and the problem.

Keep your young child in your sight during the time-out. The time-out place should be in a location that is safe, well lit, and boring. This place could be a chair or a certain corner of the room.

The length of the time-out depends upon the child's age. The general rule is one minute per year of age. This means a three-year-old would have a three-minute time-out and a four-year-old would have four minutes.

When using a time-out, state it to your child quietly. You must remain calm. This way your child knows it's time for everyone to calm down and think about what happened. For time-out to work, you must be respectful to your child. Time-out doesn't work if you are angry or threatening.

If your child doesn't want to stay in the special time-out chair or corner, calmly return him. Do this again and again until he stays. Tell him the time-out doesn't start until he stays. The sooner he cooperates, the sooner the time-out will end.

When the time-out is over, talk to your child about why he was in time-out. Explain what behavior you expect from him. Redirect him. Praise him when he behaves well.

Using Consequences

Near the end of the toddler years, you can start using consequences to discipline your child. Consequences are the results of a decision. In this approach, your child chooses her own behavior and feels the consequences of her choices. When your child misbehaves, she can learn from the results of her actions. The two types are natural and logical consequences.

Natural consequences are the natural results of a behavior. You do not have to set up these consequences—they occur on their own. See Figure 8-9. Your child can learn from experiencing the natural results of her behavior.

Natural consequences should be unpleasant enough to motivate your child to change. An example would be if you

 8-9   If your child refuses to eat, a natural consequence of this choice would be getting hungry soon after the meal.

warn your child not to treat a toy roughly. If she keeps banging the toy on the floor, it may eventually break. This might teach your child to treat her toys more gently.

One caution is needed, however. Some natural consequences are too dangerous. For instance, if your child ran into the street, you wouldn't allow her to be hit by a car. You wouldn't let her be physically harmed in any way. Instead, you would choose a different guidance or discipline method to keep her from running into the street again.

Logical consequences are those related to a misbehavior that you set up to teach your child a lesson. Suppose your child scribbles on the walls with a crayon. A logical consequence might be having her help clean up the mess. This might keep her from scribbling on the walls again.

Withdrawing Privileges

Another type of discipline is withdrawing privileges when your child misbehaves. This method works best with older children who can understand it. One option is to take away a privilege connected with the misbehavior. Calmly explain what you're taking away in a firm but helpful way. You might say, "Jacob, you threw your cars across the room. Now it's time to put them away for the rest of the day."

You can also take away a privilege that is not related to the misbehavior. This is best used for serious or intentional misbehavior. Choose a privilege that is meaningful to the child, such as watching a movie, playing with a certain toy, or going on a special outing. (Don't take away a child's comfort object.) If he misbehaves, you can warn him to stop. You might say, "The rule is no hitting. If you hit your cousin again, you can't watch that special movie tonight." Now, withdrawing the privilege has become a consequence. If he chooses to misbehave, calmly take the privilege away.

Even though your child will be upset, stand firm with your discipline. If you do what you say you will do, your child will learn you are serious. He will believe you, and be more likely to listen to you the next time.

Using Reprimands

A reprimand is a sharp statement about a child's misbehavior and the proper behavior she should use instead. A reprimand is most effective when it is not used very often. If this is your most common method of discipline, your child will soon learn to tune it out. A reprimand has the following three parts:

- ☞ a command to stop the misbehavior
- ☞ one reason the misbehavior must stop
- ☞ an alternative to the misbehavior

For example, you might say, "Stop hitting Mary. Hitting hurts. Ask Mary nicely to give you the teddy bear." A reprimand is most useful when you must get a behavior to stop right away, such as when there's a risk of physical harm or danger. For less serious behaviors, use a reprimand only after trying to guide her in other ways.

Punishment

Punishment is a penalty imposed on a person who misbehaves. Two types are physical and emotional. Physical punishment includes slapping, pushing, and spanking. Emotional punishment can include yelling, threats, and withholding love from a child.

Most family experts do not advise the use of punishment to change a young child's behavior. Punishment involves the use of adult power and control over a child. It does not teach him how to behave. Your child only learns that if he misbehaves, he will be punished. Punishment can also make your child feel like a failure and lower his self-esteem. Some types of punishment may cause him to feel shame, guilt, or anger. He might come to fear you and other adults. Figure 8-10 is a checklist regarding the use of punishment.

Spanking

Some parents believe using spanking is necessary when raising a child. They might say children need to be spanked. In the past, this form of punishment was widely accepted as one of the main ways to teach a child. Many parents used spanking to get their children to obey.

Checklist: Do I Have a Punishment Problem?

Read each statement below. Think about whether you have ever used the type of punishment described. Check the appropriate column.

	YES	NO
1. Relied on spanking to correct your child's misbehavior?		
2. Called your child *bad, stupid,* or *dumb*?		
3. Constantly nagged your child to do (or stop doing) something?		
4. Compared your child to another child?		
5. Threatened your child?		
6. Frightened or scared your child?		
7. Yelled at your child?		
8. Told your child you don't love him or would stop loving him if he didn't behave?		
9. Said negative things about your child to other adults in your child's presence?		
10. Ever felt out of control when (or just after) punishing your child?		

If you answered yes to one or more of these questions, you may have a punishment problem. Each of the parenting behaviors listed above can have a negative effect on children. Consider looking for other ways to shape your child's behavior. Read a parenting book or contact a professional if you need help or ideas.

8-10 Answer the questions in the checklist honestly to find out whether you have a problem with relying on punishment.

Today, however, research has revealed more about the true effects of spanking. Most of these effects are negative. Some of them are really harmful. It seems that spanking really doesn't accomplish what people had thought that it did. Experts now advise parents to use guidance and discipline, rather than spanking, to teach their children.

Studies show spanking has little effect on changing a negative behavior into a positive one. After you spank her, your child knows you didn't like her behavior. She may also think you don't like her, either. Spanking doesn't teach her <u>why</u> the behavior was wrong or what behavior would be better.

In addition, spanking is physically and emotionally painful for your child. During and just after a spanking, your child may be flooded with pain, anger, fear, or shame. At this time, she can't pay attention to what you are saying. She can't think about her misbehavior or feel regret.

Spanking can cause your child to have hostile, angry feelings toward you and others. She may even grow to hate the person who spanks her. This can ruin the feelings of trust and attachment you have with your child. If your child thinks you're wrong for spanking her, she may think you're wrong about other things, too. This can lead her to stop listening to you.

Frequent use of spanking can teach that it's okay to hit other people when you are bigger and stronger than they are. Your child may learn the way to control others is to hit them. This can lead your child to use violent, aggressive behavior herself.

Spanking can get out of hand if overused. It can lead to physical abuse. Many incidents of child abuse have begun with a spanking incident.

Finally, spanking does not teach your child self-control. Instead, it teaches her you will control her behavior by spanking her when she gets out of hand. One of your goals as a parent is to teach your child to control her own actions. This will help her become a safe, responsible adult. Spanking can defeat this goal.

As you can see, there are many reasons to avoid spanking your child. Guidance and discipline can work much better to shape your child's behavior. These methods also promote a healthy relationship between you and your child.

Stress in Young Children

When you think of stress, your young child is probably not the first person who comes to mind. You probably see a teen or an adult. Even your young child feels stress, though. Stress is the reaction of your mind and body to changes. Some of life's changes are positive. Stress caused by these changes is good. It can give your child energy and excitement. Having a birthday party can be a source of good stress.

On the other hand, some of life's changes are negative. These changes cause your child a different kind of stress. Too much of this negative stress can lead to feelings of helplessness. It can affect your child's well-being.

As a parent, you will want to protect your child from large amounts of negative stress. It is not possible (or desirable) to shield your child from all stress, though. If you did, your child wouldn't know how to handle stress as an adult. Instead, you can teach him how to deal with the stress he faces.

Common causes of stress are hearing others fight, changing child care situations, and changing routines. Illness, hunger, and fatigue (extreme tiredness) that last for a long time can cause stress, too. Other stressors include moving to a new home, gaining or losing a family member, and divorce.

When your child has too many stresses at once, it can start to affect him. Watch for signs of stress in your child. See Figure 8-11. Your child probably won't have all these symptoms at the same time. He may also have some signals that are unique to him. You know your child best. Trust your instinct about whether your child is feeling too much negative stress.

Signs of Stress in Young Children

Physical Signs	Behavior Signs
clenching the teeth	using baby talk
fidgeting	biting fingernails
being pale	clinging
having rigid body posture	sucking hair, thumb, or clothes
sweating	casting the eyes down
crying	twirling the hair around the finger constantly
vomiting	hoarding food or toys
headache	kicking or hitting
stomachache	making much more noise than usual
rocking body back and forth	screaming
disrupted eating patterns	stuttering
disrupted sleeping patterns	whining
having toileting accidents (after using the toilet regularly for some time)	withdrawing

8-11 Young children show their stress in many ways. Some of these are physical, while others have more to do with behavior.

How Your Child Reacts to Stress

When faced with stress, each child responds in her own way. How does your child react to stress? Watch and listen to your child carefully when she's under stress. Her reaction can tell you how she needs you to help her deal with this stress.

Some children don't outwardly show they are stressed. These children are calm and easy-going; they don't seem to be bothered by stress. They bounce back when schedules change or other stressful conditions occur. These children seem to be able to take things as they come.

If this describes your child, consider her (and yourself) lucky. When stresses build, support her ability to cope with stress on her own. Be available to talk (or listen) if she needs you, but don't hover.

Many children are more sensitive to stress. They don't respond as well to it. These children may react in various ways. Some responses are mild, while others are fairly serious. Children may become sick when they're under stress. If the stress lasts long enough, they may suffer from failure to thrive. Some children are cranky or difficult as a result of stress. Acting out and being aggressive is common. Becoming withdrawn is, too. Still other reactions include being angry, sad, grouchy, confused, or frustrated.

Children's negative reactions to stress can challenge their parents and caregivers. It may seem harder to support and comfort a child who is behaving poorly. Some parents don't easily see the link between the bad behavior and stress. By learning how your child deals with stress, you will know which behaviors are stress-related. You can prevent these behaviors by helping her cope with stress.

If your child is very sensitive to stress, she will need you to be more involved in helping her relieve it. When possible, give her plenty of warning when changes are coming. Talk with her about her fears and suggest ways she can deal with them. Give her all the extra emotional support you can.

Dealing with Your Child's Stress

Young children need help to deal with their stress. First, parents, caregivers, and other adults in a child's life can act as a buffer in stressful situations. As children get older, they slowly become better at dealing with life's ups and downs. You can use the following guidelines to help your child handle stress.

- ☞ Allow your child to have and express his own feelings. Accept his negative feelings and help him to resolve them. Even if you think the reason your child is upset seems trivial, it is important to him.
- ☞ Help your child see the positive aspects of a stressful situation. Your attitude can affect how he sees things. Viewing a situation with a positive attitude can help.
- ☞ Teach your child to relieve stress through physical activities and exercise. Running, kicking a ball, and jumping are good ways to release tension. Being physically active is good for your child.
- ☞ Balance activity with relaxation. Help your child find ways to soothe himself. Use quiet activities he enjoys. Listening to music or singing helps some children. Drawing, painting, and coloring help others relax. Holding a special toy and sleeping with a favorite blanket are comforting, too. See Figure 8-12.
- ☞ Spend more time together. In times of stress, your child needs more attention and reassurance from you. You can bond with your child by taking walks, playing quiet games, reading stories, or doing chores together. Nothing can take the place of time you spend with your child.
- ☞ Keeping a daily routine gives your young child security. It helps him know what to expect. Your child needs to know his basic needs will be met. Routines can also reassure your child that, although some things change, many will stay the same.
- ☞ Physical and emotional support help reassure your child in times of stress. Both of you may be soothed by sharing hugs, kisses, pats, cuddling, and rocking. Verbal encouragement also helps. Reassure your child that together you will get through this hard time.

8-12 When your toddler feels especially stressed, resting for a few minutes with her favorite teddy bear can help her relax.

Guiding Children with Special Needs

A child with special needs is one who needs more or different care and guidance from an average child. Children with serious health conditions have special needs. A child may also have mental or physical disabilities that create special needs. Emotional and learning disorders can also present additional needs.

If your child has special needs, you may have mixed feeling about this. When you first find out about your child's special needs, you may feel overwhelmed. A mixture of fear, anger, grief, and confusion is common. You may feel unsure what the future will hold. These feelings are normal. Many parents find talking to a professional who understands the child's special needs is helpful. A counselor can also help.

Learn as much as you can about your child's needs. Read about others in the same situation. Talk to doctors, counselors, teachers, and other parents whose child has the same needs as your child. Ask as many questions as you need to. Use the Internet to research your child's special needs and find resources, too. Learn what options are available for your child and your family. Some of these may include the following:

- ☛ special education services
- ☛ physical therapy
- ☛ counseling
- ☛ support groups
- ☛ financial aid
- ☛ health services

Take whatever steps you can to meet your child's special needs. Start as early as possible. Depending on your child's situation, there may be services available for your child soon after birth. These services can help your child reach her full potential.

Learning about your child's needs will also help you know what to expect. Parenting a child with special needs takes extra effort and dedication. It can be tiring but rewarding. Reach out to family and friends for support. Look for community agencies and support groups that can be part of your support system, too. Taking care of yourself is also important.

☛ As a parent, understanding your young child will help you guide his behavior. It will also help you know what to expect from his.

☛ Your child learns behaviors in several ways. These include imitating role models, direct teaching, trial and error, and reinforcement. Being aware of your part in the process can help you teach your child the behavior you want her to use.

☛ Enhancing self-esteem is a goal of guidance. A child with high amounts of self-esteem likes himself, feels worthy, and tries when faced with challenges. He is confident in himself and his abilities.

☞ Your child needs you to help her learn appropriate behavior. You can do this through guidance and discipline. As a result, your child will learn to tell acceptable from unacceptable behavior. If you guide and discipline her properly, she will also develop self-control.

☞ Indirect guidance involves setting up the environment so your child behaves in acceptable ways. This includes childproofing, arranging his schedule, and planning his activities.

☞ Direct guidance includes the words and actions you use to influence your child's behavior. Helping her develop self-control is a goal of direct guidance. You can use several basic direct guidance techniques with your young child.

☞ The guidance techniques you use will change as your child grows. During infancy, his ability to understand is limited. When he is older, you can use more advanced and direct techniques to guide him.

☞ Discipline includes various techniques, too. These are time-outs, consequences, withdrawing privileges, and reprimands. No matter which discipline techniques you use, you must be consistent and set reasonable limits on your child's behavior.

☞ Today, most experts agree physical and emotional punishment should not be used to change a young child's behavior. Spanking, a form of physical punishment, has several negative effects. It also has little effect on changing negative behaviors.

☞ Too much stress can have negative effects on young children. As a parent, learn about the signs of stress so you can identify them in your child. Your child needs your help to learn to deal with stress.

☞ Parents of a child with special needs should learn all they can about their child's special needs. They can find out what options are available for helping them meet these needs. Parenting a child with special needs can be tiring but rewarding.

Chapter 9
Choosing
Child Care

When your baby was first born, you may have felt a natural protective instinct. You probably trusted very few people to be near your newborn. At first, you needed to stay home and recuperate from the birth. While you were home, you probably stayed with your baby around the clock, even if a relative was staying with you to help.

A few teen parents, mostly mothers, may stay home with their children full-time. This is most common among married teens or teens who live with their parents. If you're like most teen parents, however, at some point, you'll need to complete your education or work outside the home. If you return to school or work, someone else must care for your child while you're away.

Any person other than a parent who provides routine care for a child is called a caregiver. If you are (or will be) returning to school or work, you will need to find a caregiver for your child. See Figure 9-1. Choosing child care is a big decision. There's a lot to learn. This chapter will teach you about the types of child care, what to look for in quality child care, and how to find child care.

Considering Child Care Needs

Before you start looking for child care, you'll need to assess your needs. Both your needs and your child's needs are important. When thinking about these needs, ask yourself these two questions.

☛ Why do I need child care? Identifying your goals can guide your search for quality child care. Most teen parents need child care so they can return to school or work. Reaching these goals is important for you and your child. By finishing your education, you will be much more likely to get a job that can support both of you. By working, you will earn needed income and learn job skills. Feeling good about your child care situation will help you focus on what you are doing while you're away.

☛ What are my criteria for judging child care? What do you want in the care your child receives? Most parents think about safety, cost, and convenience. You may also want a qualified, caring caregiver. Finding someone who can provide care for the days and hours you need is essential.

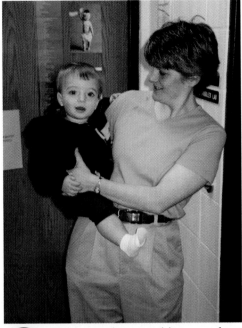

 This caregiver provides care for children each day while their parents are away at work.

You will set other criteria based upon what is important to you. You will learn more about criteria later in this chapter.

Types of Child Care

Three main types of child care are available. Many teen parents have a relative or friend who can provide child care for them. Others rely on family child care homes. Some use child care centers. Each type has advantages and disadvantages. Think about how each point relates to your own situation. This will help you decide which type of care will work best for you and your child.

Relative or Friend as Caregiver

Many teen parents choose to have a relative or friend provide child care. At first, this may seem like the perfect answer. After all, you and your child would already know and trust this person. Before deciding, though, think about your situation. No child care arrangement is perfect—all of them have disadvantages. Be honest with yourself and the other person about whether this would be the best care for your child.

Any relative or friend you choose to care for your child should have enough experience to handle the job. He or she should know a lot about children and the care they need. Choose someone who likes your child and really wants to care for her. This will help things go smoothly. Use the questions listed in Figure 9-2 to help you decide about a relative or friend as caregiver.

Most often, this type of care is provided by the child's grandparents or great-grandparents. These relatives have lots of experience, and they love your child very much. If they can, they might really enjoy caring for her. You may feel very secure with this child care agreement.

Many grandparents work, though. If so, they may not be able to provide child care. Some great-grandparents don't have the energy an active child requires. They may also have health concerns that keep them from providing child care.

Questions to Ask: Relative or Friend as Caregiver

Before you place your child in the care of a relative or friend, you will want to ask yourself some questions about this person. Be sure to answer honestly. You want to be sure this is the right child care situation for your child.

❖ Is this person in good health and able to get around well?

❖ Does this person enjoy playing with and teaching your child?

❖ Does this person have the patience and energy your child requires?

❖ Does this person respect your wishes concerning the care and discipline you expect for your child?

❖ Does this person really want to care for your child, or is he or she just doing you a favor?

❖ Would this person know what to do if your child suddenly became ill or was hurt?

❖ Would this person refrain from hitting, slapping, yanking, or scaring your child?

If your answer to all these questions is yes, this relative or friend might be a good caregiver for your child.

Ask yourself these questions about any relative or friend you are considering as a caregiver for your child.

Instead of your parent or grandparent, you might choose another relative. An older brother or sister, aunt, uncle, or cousin might be willing to care for your child. A friend might also be a good choice. This person might be another parent, an older friend, or a friend of your family.

Be sure the person you choose is committed to providing care for your child. Would this person be likely to find "something better" to do, leaving you at the last minute without child care? If so, find someone else.

Advantages of a Relative or Friend as Caregiver

Child care by a friend or relative is often pretty informal. It can be done in your home, the home of the caregiver, or both. This arrangement seems to work well for many teen parents.

Relatives and friends can provide safe, secure, and flexible care. This type of care is often the most affordable. Many relatives and friends offer their services at a low cost. Some might not charge you at all. This happens most often with the child's grandparents or great-grandparents.

You may feel more secure leaving your child with someone you know. This is a benefit of care by a relative or friend. Many children become quite close to their caregivers. It's nice when the caregiver is also a member of your family or a close friend. Your child will get to know this person well early in life. He can find comfort, love, and security in this person. This can become a lifelong relationship.

Having your parents or grandparents provide care for your child has an added benefit. You already know how this person interacts with children. You're familiar with his or her guidance and discipline. This can make you feel more comfortable with the care your child receives. See Figure 9-3.

 Both grandfather and grandchild enjoy spending time together. This type of care can be comforting for parents.

Disadvantages of a Relative or Friend as Caregiver

Care by a friend or relative can also have drawbacks. When grandparents provide care, a teen parent may start to feel they are trying to take over. This is most common when the grandparents, parent, and child live together. Grandparents have to learn their new roles. Providing care for their grandchild involves many of the same responsibilities they had as parents. This can make their roles seem unclear. You may feel confused, too. While you're thankful for their help, you want to keep your role as parent. This may cause conflicts between you and your parents.

If this starts to happen, talk with your parents about it. Share your feelings about the situation. Work with them to define your separate roles. (To learn more about this topic, see another title in this series, Understanding Your Changing Life.)

The home of your friend or relative may not have been childproofed. It may not have age-appropriate toys and equipment for your child to use in play. There may not be a safe outdoor play area available for her. This caregiver may not have a set schedule or offer learning activities for her.

Sharing child care responsibilities with a friend or relative may also change the relationship you have with this person. It may become closer, but problems may also develop.

The caregiver may start to feel taken for granted. This person may not feel appreciated for what he or she does for you and your child. Relatives and friends may feel you leave her in their care longer than needed. You may start to feel uncomfortable and indebted to this person.

A relative or friend may not listen to what you say as well as another caregiver. This person may think he or she knows more about caring for children than you do. He or she may not follow your directions as closely.

Money can become an issue between family members or friends. If you pay little or nothing, the caregiver may start to feel used. He or she may want to tell you how to spend any money you have. After all, this person is saving you a lot of money. He or she may not want to provide low-cost care if you waste your money. Of course, you may not feel comfortable with someone telling you how to spend your money. This can lead to disagreements.

Both you and the caregiver will have to make special efforts to maintain your relationship. The two of you need to work through problems that arise. See Figure 9-4 for suggestions.

Strengthening Family and Friendship Ties

When a friend or family member provides child care, problems can arise. To maintain a good relationship, be sure to do the following:

❖ Discuss how much you will pay for child care and when you will pay it. Stick to the agreement the two of you have made.

❖ Discuss your expectations. Be honest about what you expect from the caregiver. Listen to what he or she expects from you.

❖ Talk about any concerns right away before a problem builds. Day-to-day problems can become emotional when dealing with a family member or friend. Everyone will benefit from handling problems as they occur.

❖ If your family member or friend refuses to let you pay for child care, discuss what chores you could do for this person in return.

9-4 You can use these tips to help maintain a strong relationship between you and the friend or relative who cares for your child.

Family Child Care Homes

In family child care, a caregiver provides child care in his or her own home. In most family child care homes, the caregiver takes care of a small number of children—usually three to six. This number includes the caregiver's own children. Some family child care homes provide care for as many as 16 children.

Laws about child care vary from state to state. States set laws about the caregiver-child ratio. In some states, the rule is one caregiver for every six children. Providers may need to hire one or more assistants if they care for more children than this. The laws may also state how many infants and toddlers can be cared for in each family child care home. Infants and toddlers need closer supervision than older children. They also need much more personal care.

You might also look for family child care homes that are licensed. Licensing laws differ from one state to another. Some states require certain family child care homes to be licensed. Other states don't require licensing for family child care. In some states, licensing may be optional.

To get a license, providers must meet many guidelines set by the state. Some of these relate to safety, space, staff, and number of children. Licensed homes are inspected by the state to make sure the home meets all the requirements of its license. If the guidelines are not met, the caregiver can be fined or have the license taken away.

Family child care homes can also be accredited. This means they are approved by a leading agency in the field. The National Association for Family Child Care accredits family child care homes. To apply, providers must meet education and experience criteria. As part of the application process, the association observes applicants at work.

Ideally, you want to pick a licensed and accredited family child care home. This type of care isn't always available, however. If you choose an unlicensed family child care home, be sure the provider cares for only a very small number of children, including his or her own. With an unlicensed home, you must watch more closely to be sure the care is of high quality. You can tell the quality of care based on the following:

- ☞ toys and equipment available (Are they age-appropriate?)
- ☞ educational program, activities, and schedule of the home (Is it organized and appropriate for your child?)
- ☞ condition of the home (Is it spacious and clean?)
- ☞ observing the caregiver and the children together (Do they get along well?)

See Figure 9-5 for more questions to ask a family child care provider you are considering.

Advantages of Family Child Care Homes

Using family child care has quite a few advantages. First, this type of care is more homelike and relaxed than a child care center. Your child can share household and family activities with the caregiver's family.

Questions to Ask: Family Child Care

Before you place your child in a family child care home, you will want to ask the caregiver some questions. Also, look for these things as you observe the home. You want to be sure this is the right child care situation for your child.

❖ How much TV do the children watch each day? What programs are viewed and how closely is this monitored? (The American Academy of Pediatrics strongly urges caregivers to avoid TV use for children under two years of age. At most, older children should view 2 hours or less of quality children's programming per day.)

❖ What learning activities are provided for the children? Is there a weekly lesson plan written? If so, can you see it?

❖ What foods are provided for the children? Who prepares these foods? Is a weekly menu provided for the parents?

❖ When the children are outside playing, are you in the play area with them, closely supervising their play?

❖ What happens if the caregiver is ill or one of his or her own children is sick? What days does the caregiver want off for holidays and vacations? Is there a back-up person who provides care, or do you have to find your own back-up?

❖ What happens in an emergency if a child needs immediate medical attention? Who takes the child to the medical center? Who supervises the other children while the caregiver is absent?

9-5 Ask yourself these questions about any family child care provider you are considering.

Second, family child care may offer your child one consistent caregiver. (If the home has many children, there may be two or three caregivers.) He may form a close relationship with this person. This caregiver is the only other person who will provide care for him. He won't have to adjust to several caregivers.

Your child may also receive a lot of individual attention in a family child care home. When there are fewer children, the caregiver can spend more personal time with each one.

With the smaller number of children at a family child care home, your child may also be healthier. He will be exposed to fewer germs and infections than children at child care centers.

Your child will also have a few close playmates. Playing with children of all ages can teach him to cooperate and develop social skills. Since the children spend much time together, it is more like a family setting.

Family child care providers are often flexible with scheduling. They may have more or better hours available. This is good for parents who attend school or work in the evenings and weekends.

Cost is also an advantage. Family child care usually costs less than child care centers. This is an important factor for most teen parents.

Disadvantages of Family Child Care Homes

Family child care has disadvantages, too. First, there may be no other adults to back up the caregivers when emergencies occur or a caregiver is ill. Usually, each caregiver must be present every day. Each person is needed to care for the children in the family child care home. If a caregiver cannot provide care, the home will likely close for the day. Parents would have to find other arrangements at the last minute.

Second, the quality of care provided in family child care homes ranges from excellent to very poor. You will have to be a careful observer when choosing this type of care. Don't hesitate to drop by unannounced to check on the situation. If you can, avoid choosing a provider who doesn't seem comfortable with you dropping by this way.

The quality of food and the healthfulness of meals and snacks also varies from one family child care home to another. This depends on the caregiver's cooking skills and knowledge of nutrition.

A third drawback is that children come and go during the year. Often, the children in a family child care home are very close. Your child may lose friends she has played with on a daily basis. This may be a hard adjustment for her.

Many family child care providers have not received formal training or education to provide child care. Many family child care homes are not licensed by the state. These homes are not inspected, so it's your job to make sure health and safety rules are followed. Be sure there aren't too many children in the home given the number of caregivers who work there.

Family child care providers may go out of business or stop caring for children at any time. This type of care may not seem as stable or reliable as other types of care.

Child Care Centers

A child care center is a facility in which a staff provides care for young children. This type of care is not given in a person's home. It is provided in a facility that is specially designed for the care of young children. See Figure 9-6.

State laws govern child care centers. These centers are required by law to be licensed. To earn and keep this license, a center must follow state health and safety requirements. Inspections by state officials ensure that

9-6 In a child care center, your child can share learning activities with other children.

health, safety, sanitation, and staffing rules are followed. If violations occur, the state can fine the center, order the center to correct the problem within a set amount of time, or take the center's license.

Each center's license states the maximum number of children for which the center can provide care at one time. Some centers are licensed for 12 or fewer children. Others provide care for over 100 children. Centers must also follow state laws about the ratio of caregivers to children. If a center has many children, it must hire more adults to provide care for them.

Licensing is required for child care centers, but accreditation is voluntary. Child care centers seek accreditation to show parents they provide quality care. The accreditation process is different from the process for family child care homes. The group that accredits child care centers is the National Academy of Early Childhood Programs. This group is part of the National Association for the Education of Young Children (NAEYC). To apply for accreditation, a center's staff and the parents whose children attend the center must write a report. This report must tell how the center meets a list of criteria set by the Academy. After reviewing the report, the Academy sends someone to visit the center. Following the visit, a committee decides whether the program will be accredited.

If you are considering a child care center, you can ask to see its license. Do not choose a center in which no one can show you its license. You might also ask if the program has been accredited. You may feel more secure about using an accredited program.

Many child care centers offer some sort of educational program. These centers have a school-like setting. They provide learning activities for infants, toddlers, and preschoolers. At these centers, your child can choose from a variety of toys and books designed for his level of development. Many child care centers also have large outdoor play areas with safe equipment.

Fees vary from one center to another. Some are quite expensive, while others are more affordable. In some government-sponsored centers, a low income level may be an entrance requirement. Fees may be based on a sliding scale. This means a parent's fees are based upon his or her ability to pay. The fees you will pay depend mostly on the kind of center you choose.

As a rule, infant care usually costs more than care for toddlers or preschoolers. This is because infants require more individual care and attention. Some states require one caregiver for every four infants. This means a center pays more per child in caregiver wages for infants. The center passes much of this cost along to the parents in the fees it charges for infant care.

Depending on where you live, child care centers may be easy or difficult to find. Most cities have a large variety of child care centers. This gives parents more options from which to choose. Rural areas may have few centers or none.

Kinds of Child Care Centers

There are several kinds of child care centers from which you can choose. These centers fall into two main categories—nonprofit centers and for-profit centers.

Nonprofit child care centers operate to serve the public. These centers may be funded by nonprofit organizations, schools, or the government. As the name suggests, nonprofit child care centers are not out to make money. The fees they charge merely cover their operating expenses.

For-profit child care centers are funded by the owners. These centers operate to earn money (profit) for the owners. Privately owned centers and national chain centers are for-profit child care centers. Fees at these centers are usually higher. These fees must still produce a profit after covering the center's operating expenses.

The five kinds of child care centers are described in the following paragraphs. Keep in mind these are only general descriptions. Each center is unique. Even two centers of the same kind may be quite different.

Organization-Sponsored Child Care Centers. These centers are funded in part by community organizations, labor unions, houses of worship, and service agencies. These nonprofit centers may also receive some funding through government agencies or grants. This means they can charge low fees. Fees pay for the teachers' salaries

JoAnn Macander

9-7 At this school-based child care center, children from the community have the chance to form friendships and have new learning experiences.

and supplies. Some of these centers charge fees based on a sliding scale.

School-Based Child Care Centers. Some public school districts run child care centers in their buildings. See Figure 9-7. These centers may provide care for school-age children before and after school. They might also offer full-day child care for younger children in the community. Child care fees are usually lower.

Schools may also have child care centers for the children of teen parents. This type of child care allows parents to complete their education. Teachers and child care aides care for the children at these centers. Teen parents often take parenting classes during the school year. Care in these centers may be free or at a low cost.

Government-Sponsored Child Care Centers. These centers are supported through government agencies by tax dollars. Families may pay fees on a sliding scale. The state and national government pick up the additional child care costs. Government-sponsored child care centers must follow strict guidelines set by the government. As a result, these usually offer high-quality care.

Head Start is the most familiar type of government-sponsored child care center. Head Start is a child care program that is run by the government to serve low-income families. Child care centers on military bases are also run by the government.

Privately Owned Child Care Centers. Privately owned child care centers are businesses owned by one person or a small group of people. These centers offer their services to make a profit. Child care fees are often higher than at nonprofit centers. The owners need to charge higher fees. The fees must pay teacher salaries, as well as buying food, equipment, supplies, educational materials, and toys. The center may have to pay rent or mortgage payments and insurance costs, too. To stay in business, the owners must make a profit. Services vary widely from one center to another.

National Chain Child Care Centers. Some child care centers are part of a national chain that is owned by a large company. These chain centers are often operated in cities and suburban areas. Generally, a large number of children must enroll for the center to make a profit. The program, equipment, and style of these programs are set by the company that owns the chain. The quality of care provided is much the same for each center in the chain.

Advantages of Child Care Centers

Many parents like the professional, schoollike setting of a child care center. This setting seems to offer more structure, as well as a variety of learning experiences. The child care center has been designed especially for children. It may offer child-sized chairs, tables, and restroom facilities. There may be more age-appropriate play equipment and toys for your child. These factors can make a child care center appealing to her.

In a center, your child will get to know and play with a number of children on a daily basis. Most of the time, centers divide children into age groups. This allows children to play with other children their age. Your child will have many playmates from which to choose. She will also learn to interact in a group setting. This is good preparation for kindergarten.

Child care centers must be licensed. This assures a safe and healthy situation for your child. These centers often have standards for hiring caregivers. Applicants need some specific training, education, or experience in working with young children. Large child care centers may also employ kitchen staff to prepare high-quality, healthful meals and snacks. See Figure 9-8. The center rarely closes because of lack of adequate staff. Even if one or two caregivers must be absent, the center can still provide care for the children.

Disadvantages of Child Care Centers

Child care centers can have disadvantages, too. For instance, your child may receive less individual attention in a group care setting. There are simply too many children for caregivers to offer much one-to-one time.

Agricultural Research Magazine, USDA

Child care centers may offer higher quality meals and snacks than other types of providers. This is especially true when the center hires its own kitchen staff.

Many child care centers may not offer evening or weekend hours. This type of care is less flexible. You could only use a child care center if its hours matched your need.

Frequent illness is a common complaint about child care centers, especially the larger centers. Germs and infections spread easily among children. Your child may catch more colds and minor illnesses at a child care center than in other types of care.

You may also have to pay for time when your child does not receive care. Suppose your child is sick for a week and you have to keep him home. Many times, you would still have to pay fees for this week to the child care center. The center has the same costs no matter whether your child is there on a particular day. The same policy may apply if your child stays with a relative for a few weeks in the summer. To hold his slot open, you must continue to pay.

The cost may also be a disadvantage. For many teen parents, for-profit child care centers are simply too expensive. Even some nonprofit centers are costly. Some families may make too much money to qualify for government-sponsored child care. They may see this as a disadvantage.

Due to the high demand for child care, many centers have waiting lists. The demand is particularly high for infant and toddler care. Parents may have to sign up on a list and choose other care until space becomes available. This can be discouraging for them.

Criteria for Selecting Child Care

Before you start your search, think about what you want in child care. Some of your criteria may differ from other parents'. Most parents think about many of the same factors, though. These include the characteristics of the caregiver and the child care program, caregiver-child ratio, safety, and cost. Other criteria may be important to you, too. If so, include these in your decision making.

Characteristics of the Caregiver

The caregiver is the central part of any child care arrangement. You want to feel good about the care your child receives from this person. You're trusting the caregiver to care for him while you're away.

Qualified

Look for a caregiver with training in child care. This might include courses in child development, health and safety, and teaching young children. A caregiver who understands all areas of development will provide better care for your child. He or she will know what to expect from your child and can help him learn. Choose someone who knows first aid and how to keep your child safe.

The caregiver should also have experience working with young children. Choose someone who knows how to provide care for infants, toddlers, and preschoolers. This person will know how to react when certain situations arise. He or she has lots of practice.

Caring

A caregiver's personal qualities are important, too. First, the caregiver should really like children and enjoy working with them. Children can sense very well whether a person likes them. If they do not feel liked, it can lower their self-esteem.

 This woman really likes children and taking care of them. Being a caring person is a characteristic of a good caregiver.

Second, you want to choose someone who is kind and caring. This person will respond to your child in a warm way. The caregiver should take the time to answer your child's questions or meet his needs. This is important. See Figure 9-9.

You can tell much about whether a caregiver is caring by watching him or her at work. Observing the caregiver interacting with other children can help you decide. Your intuition or "gut instinct" is also valuable. Don't choose someone who makes you feel uncomfortable.

Compatible

There are two aspects of choosing a compatible caregiver. First, you want someone who can get along well with you and your children. Sometimes personality conflicts occur. If so, negative feelings could make it hard for your provider to offer quality care for your child. It could also make it hard for you to treat the caregiver in a businesslike manner.

Second, it is a good idea to choose someone who shares many of your beliefs about children and their care. You want your child to feel the standards are much the same at home as they are at child care. Pick a caregiver who uses similar types of guidance and discipline as you do. Find someone who has similar rules and handles misbehavior in a similar way. This will make it easier for your child to behave appropriately both at home and at child care.

Reliable

Child care should be dependable. You will rely on the caregiver to provide constant, high-quality care for your child. If the caregiver isn't trustworthy, this can cause great stress for both you and your child. You don't want a care situation that will close without warning or a caregiver who suddenly stops caring for your child.

Reliable care also refers to consistency. You want someone who will be consistent in guiding your child. This person should be able to provide the same kind of care every day. Search for a provider who can offer your child consistent care at all times. Use the checklist in Figure 9-10 to help you select a suitable caregiver.

Checklist: Selecting a Caregiver

Read each question below. Decide whether each question is true or false about the caregiver you're considering. Check the appropriate column for each question.

	True	False
1. Enjoys cuddling, talking to, and giving attention to babies and toddlers?		
2. Spends plenty of time holding, talking to, and playing with your child?		
3. Meets the physical needs of infants and toddlers, such as feeding and diapering, properly?		
4. Provides a safe environment for children who are learning to crawl or walk?		
5. Offers your child interesting items to look at, touch, hear, and play with?		
6. Has enough time to care for each child?		
7. Works with you to help teach your child to use the toilet?		
8. Shares your beliefs about guidance and discipline?		
9. Has enough patience to care for your child?		
10. Respects your family's religious and cultural values?		
11. Knows basic first aid?		
12. Teaches your child good health habits?		
13. Provides age-appropriate activities, toys, materials, and equipment to stimulate learning?		
14. Shows signs of openness and trustworthiness?		
15. Takes time to talk with you about your child?		
16. Helps your child feel good about himself?		
17. Obtains regular medical examinations and TB tests?		
18. Has training and experience in child care?		
19. Avoids smoking? (Many health problems such as breathing problems and ear infections are linked to secondhand smoke.)		
20. Has the energy for taking care of an active child?		

9-10 You can use this checklist to evaluate each of the caregivers you are considering.

Characteristics of the Program

If you are trying to decide between two appropriate caregivers, you may be able to make your decision based on the programs they have. The characteristics of a child care program are important to parents. You want a program with safe, adequate, and inviting facilities. Having the appropriate services for your child matters, too. Finally, you'll want to consider the hours and convenience of the child care you choose.

Facilities

Evaluate the home or building where the care is to be provided. You want to make sure there is adequate space for your child to play and learn. You want him to feel comfortable in his child care environment. As you consider each option, ask yourself the following questions:

- ☞ Is the space designed for, or adapted for, children's use?
- ☞ Is the space decorated and arranged in a way that's inviting for children?
- ☞ Are there child-sized tables, chairs, or restroom facilities?
- ☞ Is there adequate outdoor play space with safe play equipment? See Figure 9-11.
- ☞ Are there a variety of age-appropriate toys and materials for your child to use?

Bonnie Mori

 Be sure the child care situation you choose offers plenty of safe outdoor space and play equipment. Your child needs fresh air and exercise.

Services Offered

In considering child care, you want to think about the services provided. Some child care arrangements are little more than babysitting. These situations mainly offer unstructured free play time. Play is, of course, valuable to your child's learning. If this type of program suits you and your child, it could be a good option.

Other programs may offer more in the way of early childhood education. In these programs, your child would have a more structured environment. She would have free play, group storytime, art activities, lessons, and music. This type of child care challenges young children to develop to their potential.

Hours

You know the hours for which you will need child care. Choose care that is offered for the hours you need it. This will be an important factor. You might also use two different child care providers to cover the hours you need. Many parents would choose this option only as a last resort.

Convenience

You will want to choose a child care situation that is close to your home, school, or work. It should be a place to which you can walk, drive, ride, or take public transportation easily. This will make your day run more smoothly. For those who do not drive, the location is a key factor.

Caregiver-Child Ratio

Ask about the caregiver-child ratio at any home or center you are considering. If at all possible, do not choose a care situation that exceeds the state recommendation. If you can, find one with a lower ratio than that set by state law. This means more adult time and attention would be available for your child.

Safety

Having a safe and healthy environment is vital. Your child explores his surroundings with his mouth, fingers, and hands. He needs to play and learn in an area that is clean and sanitary.

Infants and toddlers require safe, clean equipment in living, playing, eating, and sleeping areas. A young child requires constant supervision. He can quickly get into danger if left unattended for even a minute.

Other safety considerations include having safety plans to cover many emergencies. For example, posting the steps to take in a fire, tornado, or earthquake can be helpful. Written safety plans for other emergencies are also needed. You can ask the provider what the procedures are in various emergency situations. This tells you whether the caregiver thinks ahead about preventing problems in an emergency.

Cost

You will need to find child care that will fit into your budget. Look at your monthly income and expenses. Is anyone, such as your parents or the baby's other parent, able to help you pay child care costs? How much are you able to afford each month for child care?

Ask what is included in the child care fee. Some providers include food, transportation, and diapers in their fee. Others do not. These providers might offer them at an added cost or expect you to provide them yourself. Knowing what is included can make it easier to compare fees between programs.

If you find you cannot afford child care, talk to your local public aid office. You may qualify for help in paying child care costs. This would help. People who already receive financial aid from the government may be more likely than others to receive this help.

Locating Child Care

Finding the right child care can be a challenge! It takes time to choose a good child care situation. Some experts advise starting to look at least six weeks before you want the care to begin. You will want to feel sure you have chosen the right care for your child.

Searching

First, identify all your options. What child care is available right now? Make a list. As you begin your search, you can use several sources to gather information. Some of these are listed on the next page.

- people you know. Ask friends, neighbors, people from your religious group, coworkers, teachers, and relatives. What child care have they used, and how did they like it? Is there anyone they would recommend? Can they help you identify any other options?

- newspaper ads. Many family child care homes and some child care centers advertise in the newspaper. If you don't subscribe to the newspaper, check it out at your school or public library.

- Yellow Pages. Many child care centers advertise in the Yellow Pages of the phone book. You will find these listed under <u>Child Care</u>. Some of the ads offer information about the center; others simply list an address and phone number. See Figure 9-12.

- professionals. Ask your health care worker, caseworker, counselor, or social worker. These professionals may be able to refer you to some child care providers in your area. They might also be able to help you apply for child care assistance if you qualify.

- resource and referral agencies. An agency that serves parents by providing them with child care information is called a resource and referral agency. Many communities (or counties) have resource and referral agencies. You may be able to find the number in the phone book. If not, ask your health care provider, counselor, or caseworker to find it for you. Child care providers in the area register themselves with resource and referral agencies. The agency may also know which providers have openings. This can be quite helpful.

9-12 You can use the phone book to gather information about the child care options available.

Interviewing

Once you have identified your options, it's time to evaluate them. You will need to contact all the providers on your list. Ask about openings, hours, and cost. You can use these questions to narrow down your options.

Then, talk to each caregiver individually. You can do this by telephone or in person. If your list is short, you may wish to meet with the caregivers in person. You might be able to combine the interview with the next step—observation. If your list is long, however, it might be better to conduct telephone interviews. This can help you quickly eliminate some options.

Even if you will have a relative or friend provide care, an interview is important. This could be an informal conversation. Talk about what each of you expects. Be very clear from the start about hours needed, cost, and the quality of care you expect. Make an agreement and stick to it. This will help things run smoothly.

Observing

Following your interviews, it's time to visit the providers you're still considering. Ask to see all the areas the children use. Visit the kitchen, restroom, child care rooms, and outdoor areas. Don't be embarrassed to ask to look around the facility. See Figure 9-13 for a checklist of items to look for on your tour.

If possible, make your visits with little notice to the caregiver. This will allow you to see things as they really are. Observe at two separate times for about two hours each time. Go while other children are there, and take your child with you. It's best to choose different times of the day. Spend some time watching what goes on. Ask questions. Look around as you walk through the caregiving area.

As you tour, watch your child's reaction. Does he seem comfortable? Observe the other children, too. Do they seem well cared for and happy? Do they seem like good playmates for your child? You will feel better about leaving your child in a place where he feels happy, loved, and safe.

If a provider won't let you observe, do not place your child in his or her care. You want a provider who is willing to let you visit anytime you wish. Anything less may be a little suspicious.

Checklist: Observing Child Care

You can use this checklist as you tour child care facilities. Read each question below and check the appropriate response.

	Yes	No
Facility, Health, and Safety		
Is the facility reasonably clean and orderly?		
Are the play areas, changing tables or bathrooms, toys, and beds sterilized frequently?		
Are electrical outlets covered with safety caps?		
Are toys and equipment in good repair with no sharp edges?		
Is there a quiet area that can be darkened for naps? Is the bedding cleaned at least once per week?		
Is there adequate space where children can play?		
Are detergents, cleaners, chemicals, and medicines in locked cabinets?		
Is there a fenced, outdoor playing area? Can the caregiver see all areas of the yard easily? Is the area safe?		
Are the children clean? (No soiled diapers or training pants)		
Is the toileting area easy for children to use?		
Program and Materials		
Do the children have a daily routine and schedule of activities?		
Do the children seem happy and involved?		
Are the snacks and meals varied and nutritious?		
Are there storybooks and picture books?		
Are there enough toys and materials for all the children?		
Does the caregiver encourage communication through planned activities such as storytelling and group play?		
Program Description		
Is the caregiver-child ratio appropriate?		
Are a variety of interesting learning activities provided?		
Are a variety of social activities and field trips provided?		

9-13 You can use this checklist as you tour each of the child care facilities you are considering.

Checking References

You need to personally check the caregiver's professional references. This is very important. Don't assume that just because there's an opening, it is a good place for your child. Have the caregiver provide at least three references, including both present and past clients if possible. Ask for full names, addresses, and home telephone numbers.

Do not trust a caregiver who cannot supply any references. This may indicate the provider hasn't been honest about past experiences or that problems have occurred between the caregiver and parents.

Call each of the references given. Ask each reference the following questions:

- ☞ When, and for how long, did this person provide child care for your child or children?
- ☞ What was your opinion of the care this person provided?
- ☞ Was this person easy to work with?
- ☞ Did your child like him or her?
- ☞ Would you recommend this person to a friend or family member?
- ☞ Did any major problems occur between you and this person regarding your child's care?
- ☞ Do you have any concerns about this person's ability to provide quality child care?

Making the Choice

By this point, you may have narrowed down your search to just one choice. If so, your decision is made; you're lucky. Otherwise, you need to evaluate all the options still on your list. Use all the information you've gathered as you make your decision. For many parents, this is the hardest part.

It may help to list the pros and cons of each option. Include all the facts about each situation. This may make one option stand out more clearly than the others. If not, list your criteria on a separate sheet of paper. Rate each situation on how well it meets each of these criteria. Is one choice the clear winner?

If you find you're still unable to choose, maybe you could ask your parents or another trusted adult for input. With their experience, they might be able to point out more factors you haven't considered. You can also visit each place once more, concentrating on how each makes you feel.

You must choose the child care situation you think will be best for your child. Once you have decided, call the provider you have chosen and let him or her know. Do this as soon as possible to make sure your child's slot will stay open. You may wish to call the providers you didn't choose, too.

Feel confident in the decision you've made. You have taken your time and carefully considered all options. Even if your child is too young to tell you so, she will appreciate the care you've taken to find her a good caregiver.

Adjusting to Child Care

The first time you leave your child in someone else's care will be an emotional experience. Adjusting to a new child care situation can be tough for both you and your child. See Figure 9-14. In time, however, you will develop a new routine that includes child care. You and your child will adjust to the changes.

It was once thought that children who were in child care would suffer from this experience. There was much debate over whether child care was good for a child's long-term development. Most studies have shown no big differences between children who were in child care and those who were not. The quality of care seems to be more important than who is providing it. As long as your child receives quality care, he will grow to meet his potential.

9-14 Your child may cling to you the first few times you take her to child care, but with your encouragement, she'll soon adjust.

Your child's reaction to child care will depend on his stage of development. With very young infants, adjusting to child care is often harder for the parents than for the child. This is because stranger anxiety has not yet developed. Your baby prefers you, but he isn't fussy when someone else cares for him for a while.

An older infant or toddler may feel very upset when he starts child care. This is normal and healthy. It shows he is attached to you. Your child may feel distress about being separated from you. He may fear you won't return. If the caregiver is a stranger, he may be afraid until he gets to know this person better. See Figure 9-15 for hints on leaving your child with a caregiver.

The changes in his schedule may be upsetting, too. It will take some time to get used to a new routine. This sense of upset may last for as long as two to four weeks. If after a month he is still upset, there could be a problem. Reevaluate your child care decision. Make a surprise visit to observe the caregiver's interaction with your child. Be sure he is getting suitable care.

Once your child is in child care, visit whenever you can and observe. Ask the provider what happens in child care each day and how your child reacts. If you don't have much time to talk with the caregiver when you drop off or pick up your child, set up a time to come in and talk.

Build a positive relationship with your child's caregiver. See Figure 9-16 for ideas. You and the caregiver are a team, working together to nurture and care for your child. The caregiver expects certain things from you as a parent. For instance, you need to be on time in picking up your child and paying. Let the caregiver know of any changes in your child's health, routine, or family living situation. This information might help him or her provide more sensitive care for your child.

Hints for Leaving Your Infant or Toddler with a Caregiver

	Child's Needs	**Parent Hints**
0 to 7 Months	Your baby needs someone to meet his needs for comfort, love, and good basic physical care.	If you start child care now, it may be more difficult for you than it is for your baby. Young babies usually adjust well to a consistent child care provider. Stay for 15 to 30 minutes the first few days. When it is time to leave, hand your baby to the caregiver. Tell your baby, "Jane will take care of you while I am at school." A calm voice and manner will reassure your baby. Describe your baby's daily routine, food preferences, sleeping habits, likes and dislikes, and the family situation. Provide this information in writing.
7 to 12 Months	This is a more difficult time for your baby to start staying with a caregiver outside the family. This is when stranger anxiety usually occurs.	Try not to start child care at this time if possible. Take a little time each day before you leave. Create a good-bye ritual and be consistent each day. Say good-bye and mean it. If you're hesitant or hang around, it tells your child you don't feel good about leaving him with this caregiver.
12 to 24 Months	This is the most difficult time to leave your child. Separation anxiety peaks. Your child may weep and cling to you as you try to leave.	Be persistent and firm as you leave. Don't come back until you are ready to either stay or take your child home with you.
24 to 36 Months	The first time you leave, your child may be frightened about being left and feel angry with you for leaving. Your child is used to your help and comfort.	Talk with the teacher about your child's eating and sleeping habits and health concerns. Share what upsets and soothes your child. The first day, arrive a few minutes early so you can sit with your child and watch what is going on. Leave with a calm face, hugs, and kisses and say "Good-bye. I'll be back this afternoon." Keep walking out. Don't linger. When you pick up your child, greet the child warmly. Express how well the child did and how proud you are. Be patient—you're helping your child learn to adjust to changes, which can sometimes be frightening.

9-15 Leaving your young child with a new caregiver can be difficult. Following these hints can make it a little easier, though.

Building a Relationship with Your Child's Caregiver

✤ Pay the caregiver on time.

✤ Respect your caregiver's rules and the agreements you have signed.

✤ Drop off and pick up your child on time. Call ahead if you'll be more than 15 minutes late.

✤ Provide the agreed upon items such as extra diapers, food, and clothing. Replace these as needed.

✤ Talk with your caregiver daily about your child and what's happening at home that may affect your child.

✤ Provide up-to-date medical information and emergency telephone numbers.

✤ Give your caregiver written notice if someone else will be picking up your child.

✤ Tell your caregiver about any changes in your child's behavior or your family situation.

✤ Notify your caregiver about any changes in your schedule.

✤ Keep your child home if he is sick. Be sure to call the caregiver if your child will be absent due to illness.

✤ Pick your child up promptly if he becomes ill at the caregiver's.

✤ Tell your caregiver if your child will be absent.

9-16 You and your child's caregiver must work together to provide the best possible care for your child. Try to build a positive relationship with this person.

☛ As you start thinking about using child care, consider what you and your child need from a child care situation. This will help you find the right situation for both of you.

☛ A relative or friend might be a good person to care for your child. This type of care is often provided by the grandparents or great-grandparents. Discuss expectations with this caregiver so you can maintain a good relationship with him or her.

☛ Family child care is child care provided in the home of the caregiver. Be careful when choosing this type of care. The quality of care given varies widely from one home to another. Good family child care is affordable, homelike, and attentive to the children's needs.

☛ A child care center is a facility that provides care for young children. There are several kinds of child care centers. These centers are licensed by the state and provide a more school-like setting. However, they may offer less personal attention for your child.

☛ When choosing child care, it is good to think about the criteria on which you will base your decision. Many parents strongly consider the characteristics of both the caregiver and the child care program. Caregiver-child ratio, safety, and cost also matter.

☛ Locating child care is a process with several steps. These are searching, interviewing, observing, checking references, and making the choice. Each step takes careful consideration.

☛ Adjusting to a new child care situation can be a difficult experience for the child and the parent. Your child may need your help to handle the stress of adjusting to child care. With time, however, a new routine will develop and your child will learn to trust the caregiver.

Glossary

A

abdominal thrust. First-aid technique used to help victim remove the object stuck in the throat or windpipe of a choking victim; also called the Heimlich maneuver. (7)

accredited. Approved by a leading agency in its field; for family child care homes this is the National Association of Family Child Care and for child care centers this is the National Academy of Early Childhood Programs. (9)

age-appropriate. Describes a toy when used by someone in the age group the toy was designed for; parents want to offer the right toys based on the child's age. (4)

allergic reaction. Response that occurs when a person is exposed to a substance to which he or she has an allergy. (2)

antibodies. Substances the body forms to help it fight diseases. (4)

attachment. Strong emotional tie a person feels toward special people in his or her life. (3)

attention span. Length of time a person can focus on one object or activity; lengthens as a child grows. (6)

autonomy. A sense a person has of being able to rely on himself or herself; independence. (6)

B

babbling. Using, repeating, or stringing together sounds; develops at about five to six months. (3)

bedtime routine. A set of activities parents use in the same way each night to prepare a child for bed. (2)

bonding. The formation of a close personal relationship. (3)

botulism spores. A type of bacteria that is sometimes present in honey and corn syrup. This can make infants very sick, so these products shouldn't be used for infants. (2)

C

caregiver. Any person other than a parent who provides routine care for a child. (9)

care label. Small tag sewn into a garment that tells you how to care for the garment. (2)

child care center. Facility in which the staff provides care for young children. (9)

childproofing. The process of adapting the home to make it safe for a child; includes doing safety checks and removing hazards. (4)

children with special needs. Children who need more or different care and guidance than average children. (8)

circumference. Distance around; doctors measure an infant's head circumference to check for proper growth. (1)

concept. A general idea formed from other information and details. (6)

consequences. Results of a decision. (8)

consistency. Responding to a situation in the same way every time it occurs. (8)

coo. Pleasant sound young babies make; one of the first kinds of vocalizing babies do. (3)

coordination. Work done together by the brain, muscles, and senses to control a person's movements. (1)

D

development. Gradual changes that take place over time as a result of growth. (1)

developmental milestone. Name for an accomplishment that signals a higher level of development has been reached. (1)

difficult. Temperament style in which a person does not adjust well at all to changes or new situations; this baby spends a lot of time crying and has an irregular routine. (3)

direct guidance. Type of guidance that includes all the words and actions a parent uses to shape a child's behavior. (8)

direct teaching. Teaching on purpose; giving clear instructions on how to do something; one of the ways children learn behavior. (8)

discipline. The process of teaching and training a child to behave in acceptable ways. (8)

disengage. Stop or avoid play; sign a baby needs a break or another kind of attention. (3)

distracting. Getting a child's attention off something; generally off a misbehavior. (8)

durable. Sturdy and long-lasting; is an important consideration when choosing clothing for a toddler. (5)

E

easy. Temperament style of a person who adjusts quickly and easily to changes and new situations; this person is usually cheerful, active, happy, and regular in routine. (3)

emergency. An illness or injury that requires immediate medical help and temporary first aid. (7)

emotional development. Type of development that includes learning to express and handle feelings. (1)

empathy. Having an understanding response to the feelings of another person. (6)

engage. Enter play and share; a sign your baby is ready to learn. (3)

environment. All the effects from a baby's surroundings, including home, family, and community. (1)

F

failure to thrive. Condition caused when a child is not given enough love and attention; can affect all areas of growth. (3)

family child care. Type of child care in which a caregiver provides care for children in his or her own home. (9)

family child care home. Home in which family child care is provided. (9)

fever. A body temperature that is above the normal range for a particular person. (7)

first aid. Temporary care given immediately after a serious illness or injury until medical help arrives. (7)

fluoride. A mineral that is good for the teeth but should not be swallowed in large amounts. It is included in toothpastes. (1)

Food Guide Pyramid. A simple-to-use guide for healthful eating. (5)

Food Guide Pyramid for Young Children. A version of the Food Guide Pyramid that describes the food needs of children ages two to six years. (5)

food jag. Describes a period in which a child demands to be fed only one or two foods and refuses to eat all others. (5)

for-profit child care center. Type of child care center funded by its owners and operated to make a profit; includes privately-owned and national chain child care centers. (9)

G

guidance. The process of directing, supervising, and influencing a child's behavior; can be direct or indirect. (8)

H

handedness. The preference to use one hand more than the other for tasks; develops during the toddler years. (5)

Heimlich maneuver. First-aid technique used to help victim remove the object stuck in the throat or windpipe of a choking victim; also called the abdominal thrust. (7)

heredity. The sum of the traits parents pass to their children. (1)

hygiene. Refers to personal cleanliness. (5)

I

imitating. Copying the actions of another person; one way children learn behavior. (8)

immunizations. Special medicines given to protect a person from serious illnesses; can be given as an injection, tablet, or liquid. (4)

indirect guidance. Type of guidance that involves changing a child's surroundings to shape his or her behavior. (8)

infancy. Period of life from birth to the first birthday. (1)

infant feeder. Tube with a plunger on one end and a nipple with a large hole on the other end. This device is not recommended for use in feeding. (2)

intellectual development. Type of development that includes progress in the mind and its thinking abilities. (1)

iron-enriched. Describes a substance to which iron has been added. (2)

L

large motor skills. Skills involving the use of the large muscles. (1)

large muscles. Muscles of the neck, trunk, arms, and legs. (1)

limits. Rules a parent sets to protect and discipline a child. (8)

logical consequences. Consequences parents set up to teach their child not to use a certain behavior; these consequences are related to the misbehavior. (8)

M

minor injury. An injury that is less serious than an emergency. It is one for which an average person can easily provide care. (7)

N

natural consequences. Consequences that result naturally from a behavior. (8)

neurons. Special type of brain cells. (1)

nonprofit child care center. Type of child care center that operates to serve the public; includes organization-sponsored, school-based, and government-sponsored child care centers. (9)

O

object permanence. The ability to understand that an object still exists even if it can't be seen. (3)

over-the-counter (OTC) medicine. Type of medicine that can be bought without a prescription from a health care provider. (7)

P

pediatrician. A doctor whose specialty is caring for babies and children. (4)

physical development. Type of development that includes changes in the body and its abilities. (1)

prescription medication. Type of medicine that must be ordered by a health care provider and bought in a pharmacy. (7)

punishment. Penalty imposed on a person who misbehaves. (8)

R

redirect. To shift a child's attention from a misbehavior to a new activity. (8)

reinforcement. A parent's response to a child's behavior; can increase or decrease the chance that a behavior will be repeated; one way children learn behavior. (8)

reprimand. A sharp statement parents make about a child's misbehavior and the behavior that should be used instead. (8)

resource and referral agencies. Agency that serves parents by providing information about child care and registers area child care providers. (9)

role model. A person whose actions are copied by others. (8)

S

self-care skills. Skills that let a person provide physical care for himself or herself; such as hand washing, hair and tooth care, bathing, toileting, feeding, and dressing. (5)

self-control. The ability to resist the impulse to use inappropriate behavior. (6)

self-esteem. A person's feelings of confidence and satisfaction in himself or herself. (8)

separation anxiety. Tension a baby or young child feels when separated from a parent; may include crying, fussing, clinging, protesting, and being quite unhappy. (3)

Shaken Baby Syndrome (SBS). Serious condition in which a baby or young child has been violently shaken; can lead to disability or death. (4)

sliding scale. Payment arrangement in which cost for a service is determined by a person's ability to pay; available in some child care centers. (9)

slow to warm up. Temperament style in which a person takes time to adjust to changes and new situations but later "warms up" after being exposed to them for a while. (3)

small motor skills. Skills involving the use of the small muscles. (1)

small muscles. Muscles of the eyes, hands, feet, fingers, and toes. (1)

social development. Type of development that includes learning to relate to others. (1)

soft spots. Places in a baby's skull that are not completely fused; allowing for delivery and early brain growth. (1)

stimulation. Any kind of action or experience that prompts the brain to form a connection; necessary for brain development. (1)

stress. The reactions of a person's mind and body to life's changes. (8)

sudden infant death syndrome (SIDS). the unexpected death of a baby who seems healthy. The baby stops breathing for no clear reason, usually during the night. (2)

synapse. Connection that forms between two neurons in the brain; allows the brain to perform functions, such as thinking and coordinating the body's movements. (1)

syrup of ipecac. An over-the-counter medicine most often used to cause vomiting after a poisoning has occurred. (7)

T

temperament. A person's typical response to surroundings; part of the personality. (3)

temper tantrums. Outbursts of negative emotions and behavior that are common in the toddler years. (6)

time-out. A discipline technique that involves placing a child who has misbehaved in a quiet place for a few minutes. (8)

toddler. A child from age one to age three years. (5)

trial and error. The process of trying something in new ways until finding one that works; one of the ways children learn behavior. (8)

W

weaning. Helping a baby switch from the breast or bottle to a cup for feedings. (2)

well-child exams. Another name for the routine medical checkups toddlers and other young children need. (7)

window of opportunity. The time when the brain is best able to learn a certain skill. (1)

Index